D1617488

Winging Home

Winging Home

a palette of birds

Harold Rhenisch

illustrations by Tom Godin

BRINDLE
& GLASS

Library and Archives Canada Cataloguing in Publication
Rhenisch, Harold, 1958-
Winging home : a palette of birds / Harold Rhenisch.

ISBN 1-897142-12-9

1. Birds--British Columbia--108 Lake Region.
2. Bird watching--British Columbia--108 Lake Region.
I. Title.

PS8585.H54W54 2006   C814'.54   C2006-900775-6

Canada Council **Conseil des Arts**
for the Arts **du Canada**

Brindle & Glass is pleased to thank the Canada Council for the Arts and the Alberta
Foundation for the Arts for their contributions to our publishing program.

Brindle & Glass is committed to protecting the environment and to the responsible use of
natural resources. This book is printed on 100% post-consumer recycled and ancient-forest-
friendly paper. For more information, please visit www.oldgrowthfree.com.

Brindle & Glass Publishing
www.brindleandglass.com

1 2 3 4 5 09 08 07 06

PRINTED AND BOUND IN CANADA

for Diane, Leandra, and Anassa

❧ ❧ ❧

Keep a green tree in your heart and perhaps a singing bird will come.

→Chinese Proverb

Table of Contents

List of Illustrations ⟩ xiii

A State of Mind ⟩ 1
The Robins Come Home ⟩ 11
The Blackbird Jug Band ⟩ 33
The War Over the Muskrat House ⟩ 61
The Eagles of Sepa Lake ⟩ 95
Colonel Watson's Swallows ⟩ 127
Jokers ⟩ 167
Travellers ⟩ 185
Woody and Winston ⟩ 217

About the Author and Illustrator ⟩ 242

List of Illustrations

Black-capped Chickadee ↛ iv

European Starling ↛ viii

Great Blue Heron ↛ xiv

American Robin ↛ 11

Red-Winged Blackbird ↛ 33

Canada Goose ↛ 60

Bald Eagle ↛ 94

Cliff Swallow ↛ 126

Common Raven ↛ 166

Black Tern ↛ 184

Pileated Woodpecker ↛ 216

Barred Owl ↛ 241

A State of Mind

Old birds are hard to pluck.
     ❂German Proverb

On the top of the Central Plateau, the aspens flash and flare in wind, and the blackbirds ride the reed stalks on lakes formed entirely by snow and rain. There are twenty-five hundred lakes within an hour's drive of my house, reflecting the sky from closed-off valleys and shallow stone pans. Their water is glass among the jewel-headed fall grasses. Above them, the air hangs like a raindrop. The light is mercury. Everything is slow. Everything is happening at the same speed, which is no speed at all. ❂

We came through town in the summer, a sweltering night before Diane was interviewed for the job of principal of the junior high school. Trucks were gearing down like jackhammers on the hill coming into town from the north—right outside our hotel window—and continued all night. There was no question of sleep. For half an hour my infant daughter, Leandra, and I sat on the dew-wet and weedy grass at the side of the highway and watched the trucks pass, north and south, one a minute. With every truck Leandra yelled out in joy. I waved at the drivers. Dust scattered over us as each load passed. The whole time, lightning flared, soundless, distant, in a ring around us, now to the north, then the south, and to the west and east, yet in town the air remained dry and hot. With each arc-flash of light, huge thunderheads sprang up on the horizon, then vanished again into the dark. Only later, as I held Leandra against my shoulder and walked her back and forth in the parking lot, as a cold breeze sprang up and I sang amidst the barking of the dogs at the cattle ranch behind the hotel, did she sleep.

At breakfast, the waitresses, girls just out of high school, with white lace blouses and perfect hair, were whispering in a group around the coffee machine. Occasionally one of them drifted away for a moment to wait on a table—the restaurant was crowded—but that was obviously not the focus of their interest. Many people sat waiting without menus—like us. There was a crash of plates in the kitchen and an exclamation like a frog being eaten by a duck, followed by a short burst of laughter from the tables. The waitresses looked up briefly, then started whispering again. Finally, a blue pickup covered in mud pulled to a stop up front and a young man dressed in mud-caked jeans and workboots swung out of the box, laughed to his friends in the cab, and walked in through the people waiting for tables. He had the swagger and confidence of a young man in a town where the future belongs to young men. He said something to the girls, pointed to the truck, and our waitress wiped her hands on a towel and stepped outside. While she was gone, talking to the driver through the open pickup window, the young man inside the restaurant teased the other waitresses. They hung smiling off his every word. After five minutes our waitress kissed the driver quickly and came back in, the first young man waved and strode back out through the still swinging door, hopped into the truck, slapped the window, and the truck swung away in a roar, spitting up gravel, faces grinning out of its windows. It was a complex mating ritual, like a grouse drumming dust during a mountain afternoon. First jobs after high school: cutting down trees; serving food. What I remember is that swagger. It was not a young man who came in that door, but a god. ⇒

I didn't know then that thunderheads crack and snap overhead almost every summer afternoon on the Plateau. All day, the hot, dry air draws water out of the lakes by the freightcar load. At night, wind rages across the shores, and in the dark the pines sway twenty feet at the crowns. Caught by the wind and springing back, they leap upwards with a roaring, rustling, female cry. The storms come so regularly that to live on the Plateau is like living in the tropics, where you can set your watch by the noon rain, except that in the tropics dark comes like a curtain at 6:00 PM. In the summers here, it comes at 10:30, and is gone again by 4:00. To live on the Plateau is to live in light. Storms here smell of primal elements: water, ozone, air. The rain splashes against the windows and across the whole Plateau. Purified of the fish scent of the lakes, it lashes into the pines: primal. When the storms quiet, a flash of mosquitoes rises over the mirrored surface of the water, like chips of glass come alive, and spreads out through the trees. It butts up against windows in a high, thin whine, like the sound of nerves, the only sound you hear in an otherwise perfectly silent room. ⇒

*W*e left Keremeos in late summer, with apple harvest, grape pressing, and two and a half months of lingering Indian Summer ahead of us, two and a half months during which the days were going to slowly cool into a luminous, grey desert rain that experience taught us would join sand and sky into a watery light. Later in the day, we arrived on the Plateau. It was mid-fall. A few frost-shattered yellow leaves, half-brown from a mid-August frost, still hung on the aspens. A few woodland birds were foraging for saskatoons and snowberries. There were no birds over the water. The seedheads of the wild grasses along the paths were like feathers and bottle brushes and cotton swabs. It was a brown world. Everyone walking along the lake carried a small bell and shook it from time to time to scare off bears. A cold wind blew off the waves. ⤍

$\mathcal{H}$alfway north to the Plateau, I found myself winding down the cutbacks—thirteen percent grade for fifteen kilometres—slowly, behind a cement truck making a return trip from the copper sulfate lakes of the Highland Valley Copper Mine. The Thompson Valley was seared, brown and broken and burnt, a thousand yards and almost vertically below me, as the engine of the U-Haul roared and the transmission let out a high-pitched whine. I had a lot of time to think there, as the truck and I twisted together down the paved-over range-trail. Minute by minute there were fewer trees, but the transmission still protested. On that last stretch of road down into Ashcroft I considered the wisdom of my wife's father, Aksel, who had pointed to the map and named this lonely mine road a "good, straight, fast highway."

One minute earlier, Aksel had passed me on the near vertical drop of a hill; he had slowed down beside me to smile and wave before pushing on ahead with my deep-freeze and mattresses, past the cement truck, into the burning throat of the valley. Soon he became only the glow of a taillight two kilometres ahead. Diane was an hour behind us, with the girls: Anassa, who was six, and Leandra, a year and a half. I was alone with my thoughts. They were jammed to the door and the ceiling for twenty-eight feet behind me—all my books packed into wine and whiskey, hydro-cooled carrot and anti-freeze boxes, a piano, a pump-organ—and, you know, it felt like every one of my thoughts had achieved form there, like the antlers of a caribou, long and beautiful in the pale blue air, with the wind blowing right through them and smelling of the stars. I was carrying with me all the hope and promise of twenty years of poetry and eleven years of marriage. A lemming might throw itself off a cliff there, but I was winding down it slowly, so very slowly, as the first alfalfa fields burned like emeralds in the weeds and cattle-trodden bunchgrass, pondering the wisdom of maps. ✦

*A*ll fall I sat on the deck and looked out over the lake—as if it was a palette in Monet's hands. I set myself the task of coming to know the water colour by colour. Thirty-four years in the Similkameen had given me a knowledge of every stone, every plant, every stretch of river, every shade of light over the faces of the mountains as the snow rode lower and lower down the cliffs week after week, and though it was at times difficult not to parody that knowledge, it was a bedrock, and what I wrote stood always on what I had written before. On the Plateau, I didn't have that. I had nothing. I felt that if I was to write here I would have to get past the idea of water, past the idea of the colour blue, and find a new palette to form the foundation of a new knowledge.

Afternoon after afternoon, when Leandra slept, I left my unpacked boxes and stepped out into the air to write the colours of the lake. From apricot to sulphur to the baked enamel of heavy machinery to the hair of highland cattle and water lying over the facets of pyrites in granite, they shifted minute by minute. By the late afternoon the easterly winds had driven most of the light against the reedy west shore. It lay there in bright blue and silver chips, bobbing on the surface like fallen leaves. I wrote it all down. I recorded it in long columns, and annotated them with notes about the weather, the birds, and the wind in the trees. I thought I was writing poems.

I look at them now—my palettes of tree and reed bed and pine, shifting day by day, week by week, and although they are beautiful—

and some of the colours of lemon almost unbelievable—they remain only as what they were in the first place: palettes. And I might think that the paintings were never made from those colours, but that would be wrong, for I made them within myself and saw, for month on month, the whole landscape as a series of oils and watercolours—including every wash and every brush stroke.

At some point, somewhere, that long attention to water sank in, for week by week I felt myself stilling from the madness of moving, until one week I walked out in a bitter wind that was like the blue main current of a stream overhead, drawing all heat out of my hands. Leaves lay thick over the path in a tunnel of aspens. It was like a scene out of Robert Frost: "Two paths diverged into a wood. . . ." As I walked into the trees, a sapling suddenly rose up beside me in a stream of electric and platinum fire, and held there, trembling in the air. Then Leandra screamed and I was drawn away, giving one last glance to the sapling as I picked her up and carried her back to the house, but the moment remained there, as a suggestion that I was waking from a long and troubled sleep.

The next day, a flaming yellow sparrow flitted among the heavy branches of a willow hanging to the ground among the thistles and roses. Behind it, the lake was a sheet of shale, cut off hard and ash-grey over the shallows and broken up into little boats of light among the green canes of the new reeds. In that light, the reeds were not individual stalks but a thin cloud of colour floating just over the surface of the water. The rain streamed down incessantly. The lake's cut face sparkled with every raindrop, even those a kilometre away.

To carry the work of building a home for myself forward into the community, one lettuce-green Cariboo evening I drove into 100 Mile

House to join the local writers' group. It would give me someone to talk to. That's where I met Susan.

Susan writes women's novels. I glanced at her across the plywood table in the back room of the library. She was framed against old National Geographics from the 1920s set on shelves against the varnished plywood walls. Her hair was done up in tight curls, in a globe around her head. Her eyes were piercing, her lips thin. She had a way of throwing out her words when she talked, and of tossing her head with the rise and fall of her sentences—every movement she made was sharp and clipped. I was the odd one out there. I write poetry. I was a little nervous, and my voice quavered with it. "Poetry" elicited only silence. It was not writing.

"What's a women's novel?" I asked.

"Oh." A shake of the head. The blue eyes. A small laugh. "You know. Relationship novels." She was a little embarrassed. Susan had an agent in New York, to whom she had paid $75 US to market her historical fantasy on the Shroud of Turin.

"Your book is very publishable . . ." the agent wrote back. Susan was proud. That night in the library she asked to read us a section of her new novel about Scheh erazade. Her Scheherazade was a girl in a harem, fiercely intelligent, fussing over the shape of her breasts in a mirror, cynically jealous of the other girls there. Her Scheherezade was a princess, denied access to men, except the eunuchs—the ultimate in safe sex—whom she mentally undressed. She watched every movement of their muscles ripple under their thin, silk trousers. Their chests and backs were black and bare. Susan's tongue licked over her lips as she read. Her cheeks were flushed.

I had been in the Cariboo for two weeks. I drove home in the inky darkness. The stars splashed out over the night sky like wildflowers—

seeds cast by hand over the low meadows of the land. The land was awake, watching.

All night I dreamed about old Constantinople, and the harem. All night Susan licked her tongue over her lips. All night the eunuch stood in the doorway, to wait on a young girl's pleasure, knowing he had been called there only to be watched. All night the plywood walls. ⇒

"Where does the Cariboo begin?" asks Bob next door, the dentist, who moved here from Nanaimo a year before I arrived.

"Well . . ." I answer, stalling, giving myself time to think. Bob is tinkering with a video camera, trying to remember how to operate it. It is his daughter's ninth birthday and the candles are being lit. "It's not Cache Creek," I say. "That's the Thompson. But it's not far from there. It must be that auto-wrecking yard just north of Hat Creek, with the collapsing fence. The one that's for sale. *Land and Business.*"

The auto-wrecking yard is an architectural triumph: rough-cut wooden slabs stand up on end surrounding a field of pigweed. Across the highway, cut into the soapstone and shale, a cedar house, transplanted from the suburbs of Vancouver in the dark-stained back-to-the-land images of 1973, advertises worms and fishing information. The yard is a collection of rusted cars, used oil tanks, and moose antlers. Nothing in the yard is alive.

"You're right," laughs Bob. "It'll be a long time before they sell that one." He notices a flashing red light on the front of the camera and then dips his head to peer into the viewfinder. "That's the funny thing. You can't easily say where it begins, but when you're there, you know." The candles are all lit. Bob swings the camera around and we sing, on tape. Bob's daughter blows out all the candles—except one. It burns like a small flower cupped between her hands on a winter night. All the girls laugh. Bob's daughter blows out that last candle. The red light keeps flashing. ⇒

The Cariboo is not a place but a state of mind. In the fall the rusted tangles of junk in the ranch yards among the jackpine and the alkali lakes are covered with the heart-shaped sulphur-yellow leaves of the trembling aspens. In the late spring the willow cotton drifts and catches like snow among the pink petals of the roses. The clouds graze overhead, like electronic dreams and memory grids of water. They pass over the hills and trees of the Plateau: huge structures of consciousness ten kilometres above us. Every thought arches between the clouds in wave-signals kilometres long. ⇒⇒⇒

The Robins Come Home

God gives every bird his worm,
but he does not throw it into the nest.
>Swedish Proverb

The robins arrive on the Plateau in the greyest days of the year, when the snow has lain among the trees and houses so long you know for certain it will never, ever melt away. In March here, a half hour above the coiling, grey-green current of the Fraser River, it is impossible to picture a world not completely covered with and darkened by snow.

Darkened. Postcards show bright white snow, twinkling in the sun, looking as if the stars have fallen to earth. We get snow like that here, too, but those are December postcards, not March ones. March snow is not bright. In March, all the light in the spreading sky drains away and is caught in old, icy drifts. Frozen to their core, the trees have grown black and heavy. Their shadows are purple. Photographs of blackbirds feeding in the yellow manes of the sunflowers the previous summer, or snapshots of crabapples, glowing fuchsia pink on fall branches of yellow leaves, seem impossible here in March. They look like fakes. When you see them, you swear their colours were painted in by a child with a paint set picked up on the sale table at the nearest dollar store: *Made in China* ®. The colours are like delicate petals on tissue flowers. You feel as if you could walk through them.

To live on the Plateau in March is like having an old two-channel television with rabbit ears, while the kids down the road spend their afternoons spread out on the plush carpet, eating Cheezies, watching cartoons in full colour on YTV. On cable. That's how our winters end here: they fade away. They drizzle. They crush. March skies are as heavy as lead. You crimp them to your ten-pound-test line and drop them into the deep pools. You wait for something big to bite.

Earlier in the winter, our lives on the Plateau are full of light. We move through the winds off the sun like salamanders shifting in the coals of a fire. What everyone says on the Plateau is "Don't go south in March." It's good advice. The reason is obvious, though you usually only remember it when it's too late: while our March skies are grey and marbled with cloud, like old mop water sudsed with soap, it's not so everywhere. Six hours of *No Passing* lanes and semi-trailers south down the continuous thread of cold of the Fraser River takes you to the river's mouth, twenty-five hundred kilometres from the Rockies. By the time you have reached the coast there, you have passed with the river and the roar of the trains through the pine forests of the Plateau, the alders and cedar of the low country, and the paint-box pig farms and suburbs of the Fraser Valley. Your children call out excitedly as the trains wind across cliffs of water-worn rocks stacked up by glaciers for a thousand feet above the river. They count the coal cars: 105, 106, 107, 108. . . .

In March we follow our cold down to the sea, and there at the river's death, among the red-barked logbooms, sushi bars, and pale green glass streetfronts of Richmond and Delta, the houses barely rise above tideline. They are like boats tied up to shore, knocking at the dock. Among them, the March flowers are nodding, yellow, in thick new grass, tossed by a fresh wind off the strait. After that shock treatment of colour it is very hard to drive back home in the muck and the black ice, with all the yellow lines worn completely off the roads by winter grit, and with the tracks of avalanches still white in the gullies at the roadside. ⇨

That's March. In the dead of winter, though, in January and February, the bluebottle skies above the heaving, seasick forests of the Plateau are like a Siberian shaman's spirit stone. The world glows in those months. It is a jewel. When storms come, and they do, with irrepressible speed, they are weightless. You feel energy drain out through the soles of your feet, and then the weather is on you. Wild storms surge off the thirty-foot swells of the open Pacific and collide with the Coast Mountains, washing Bella Coola a little further off of its gravel delta into its fjord, nourishing the moss on cedar-shake roofs in the retirement communities along the east coast of Vancouver Island, and buffeting the cities clustered like purple mussels at the mouth of the Fraser. When the winter storms come to Vancouver, they spray over the cliffs at Wreck Beach, fly up in spume and foam, and land heavily on the city. They break trees over cars, scatter oak and elm branches over streets in torrents of smoky rain smelling of kelp and oysters, and drive rain horizontally into people's faces and windows. The city drums. A small river runs down each side of every street, disappearing with musical bell sounds into the storm sewers. ⇨

When the rain turns to snow, the cities slow to a crawl, and even stop. A day's drive and four cups of coffee to the north, the same storms curl off the face of a wall of pure cold that stretches from the steel-hard ground up to the upper limits of the atmosphere and the glittering stars. When the storms hit the minus-fifty-degree cold, they climb vertically to get over it, until they can rise no further and collapse as snow. The storms literally avalanche off the wall of cold, and bury Lytton and Boston Bar and Kanaka Bar: small, lost towns deep in the Fraser Canyon. Avalanches slalom down the steep cliffs, blocking the roads and the trains with packed snow and rocks and mud and splintered trees. All that time, though, here on the Plateau, the only new snow is the little that condenses out of the daytime evaporation in the dry air. The air is so cold it feels like a liquid. Nothing in the world moves, and trees, air, mountains, and snow are all the same stillness. They become one seamless substance. In that frozen world, a few people and cars make their way to and from town. They seem to be moving through a different earth entirely, one that has nothing to do with the stillness that surrounds them.

When I step out from my house into that cold, it is as if I am moving through myself, or through my memories. The world just does not seem real. Only my body is real. The year that came before, with its loons and red-billed mergansers, its twelve thundering months of Alaskan tourists, Overwaitea trucks, lumber trucks, army-fatigued hunters with the dead strapped to their roofs or cut up with chainsaws and boxed in the backs of their pickups, with its weekend traffic racing from Prince George on the nine-hour haul to Vancouver, is completely wiped clean.

After that sense of being lifted up into the weightless air, the grey skies of March add more gravity to the earth. My legs grow heavy. My thoughts are dragged to the ground. Patches of mud and trampled grass rise out of the drifts. The aspens stand around aimlessly, leafless, without snow, in a light so low across the ground it comes in like a wind. It is impossible to remember that the world was ever green. You know it wasn't. You know you are living in a ruin. To live those grey, those pressed-felt-glove March days, is like trying to sleep with a heavy wool blanket laid across your mouth. Your dreams are terrible. ✦

It is night. The forest is very dark. You enter it alone, without a light. In the absolute darkness a fish walks beside you. Through the yew trees, you reach out to touch her. She is very cold. You touch your skin with your fingers and realize that you, too, are very cold: you are a deer with tall antlers and human hands. As you brush your fingers against the branches, in the black thickets of the alders, as the tiny brown cones shake down over you and over the spiny, frill-necked rock cod who walks at your side, the air fills with a pale blue light. There are faint stars in the sky, and a terrible yellow wind raging out of the black firs on the eastern hills. Wind is already blowing before it, over the grass and the face of the lake. ⇀

You wake up aching and unrested, as if you have been going over unfinished business in your head all night long. You have. Dogs have been barking in long chains through the snow: first one dog started up, then another dog a half kilometre away through the aspens and firs picked up the call, and on and on, from house to house among the trees, and people woke and fell asleep with it, so that at all times there was someone awake in the night, listening, and someone else with dogs in his or her dreams. By the time morning rises in a pink shadow to the east, no one is rested. The people in town, walking through the old grey snow, their footsteps crunching on the sand spattered over the sidewalks for traction, are ashen-faced, and no-one believes any longer in a future. You endure.

Into this leaden world of grey aspens, grey snow, grey faces, and grey sky, the robins come one day, unannounced, their rusty breasts the first splash of colour in the world. Suddenly people have something to talk about again, other than ritual complaints about the weather. Suddenly they notice the yellow light, which has been rising, unnoticed, within the air. Even the trees take on a clarity and translucency. They no longer look frozen. They look as if they are made of light. They look like tall beer glasses full of sap. You are suddenly filled with an irrepressible happiness. You are drunk. ⤻

The robins come without a sound. It is always late afternoon, and the heat has just started to fall out of the air—it is the time of day when the light has been swept aside like a bride's veil before the altar. There are no longer any shadows at that time of day, and there is a breathless transparency to the world. The sky arches over the pale, threading limbs of the aspens in a glimmering green sheen, like a taut bridge carrying traffic out of a city into the suburbs, suspended by cables and mathematics; it spreads clear and high and elusive over the Plateau, touching the earth at the horizon and rising to tremendous height overhead. It is like the Milky Way—not the old starry Milky Way, so full of dreams and age and memories of old sci-fi novels, but a Milky Way spread out in a broad wash, like pollen blown from a flower. I have spent hours out there in the windless floor of the air, tiny among the tarnished silver trunks of the aspens as the Cover Girl light of the sunset faded out of their trunks. All the movement of the air was far above me, like breaking waves tossing around the hulls of tankers, the screws leaving long white wakes and the diesels thudding, while I scuttled with the crabs on the floor of the continental shelf, picking over scraps. It is the best time of the day to be outside. The air is clear. You go clear with it. ⤻

As the winter progresses, from the first big flakes of snow falling like promise to the six inches of ice packed down on the driveway and the glacier easing down the steps, the house grows stuffy and tight. On those first winter days, when the outside air has the sharp bite of newly forged iron and the cold moves through my whole body with each breath, it is the dust sizzling up in the heating ducts that gets to me.

By Christmas, when the stars are just above the treetops and the trees stop all movement and the air smarts of ozone, inside the house the air is stale, breathed and re-breathed until it has lost almost all its oxygen. When we add to that the high thin sting of the spruce tree in the corner, the air catches at the backs of our throats.

This is just the beginning. From the third week of February, the petroleum smell of fermenting apples rises from the cold room and seeps through the whole house. By the beginning of March, we pass the door to the cold room with tears in our eyes. Our throats go raw, as if they were rasped by thistles. It hurts to speak. It burns to breathe. Gone are the deep breaths of November and the new oxygen coursing through the bottom of the lungs. Breaths are shallow in early March, barely stirring the old dead air in the lungs. In their bins downstairs, even the good apples, shrunken and shrivelled down into themselves, have converted all their starches to sugar, and much of that sugar to alcohol, or worse, to turpentine, kerosene, even benzene. The house that such a short time ago floated on the edge of the lake like the ship of history cresting in storm has become an industrial dump.

One day, it all begins to stink too much, and I go down and sort the good apples from the bad, although with their brown, shrivelled skins, they would all pass for bad down at the supermarket. I lift the good ones into boxes, and toss the bad ones into buckets for the robins. They splash. I lift the good apples gently, cradling them like peaches in the palm of my hand, because at that age in an apple's life the lightest touch of my fingertips will be a liquid brown bruise within a week. Not that the robins mind. They prefer the rotten ones, the yellow and speckled ones, the brown, crushed ones blooming with blue-green mould and red spore bodies.

There are more bad apples than good ones. When I have finished sorting, I carry the bad ones out across the small river of melting snow that was my driveway once, and throw them over my potato patch. Day by day the apples pile up, splashes of colour on the snow. ⇥

*A*nd then the birds come. One late afternoon, as I step out to clear my head in the air that is beginning to smell faintly again of forests and the distant sea, the branches of the wild belt of trees running to the west of the house are alive with robins. The robins sit on the aluminum and charcoal branches like fruit—not a still life like the bowl of apples on a rough wooden table which Cézanne painted in Arles, but animated fruit, fluttering and moving about. The robins shift on their twig legs. They ease their beaks. They watch. It is as if in them the spirit of the trees has condensed out of the air, as if the trees' ability to move and dance has also been purified and concentrated, and the robins are its form.

The robins swoop down over my purple-skinned crabapple trees and the red-osier dogwoods I dug out of the moose swamps a kilometre to the north, and scallop into my garden with wings outstretched and every feather extended. They hop from apple to apple across the snow, then spread their legs wide and dip their heads into wells the falling apples have made in the drifts. All around them, the bright yellow balls of apples lie like Easter. The robins raise their heads to swallow after each bite, their entire bodies trembling with joy. ⇥

*A*lthough life really is that good, death is still near—even in my garden. All the time that the robins cluster among the apples, the cats prowl up and down the muddy driveway beside them, their tails twitching and their nerves on edge. The cats know they can't get at the birds, for the eight inches of soft, old snow will not hold their weight. For their part, the robins, with their perfect stereoscopic vision, know very well that the cats are there. They are just not bothered by them, that's all. They know what the cats know: that the soft snow might as well be a canyon a hundred yards wide, with the cats lining up to plunk their loonies into a coin-operated telescope to get a peek across. As the cats growl and mewl uncontrollably beside the robins, sometimes as close to them as one impossible yard, the robins continue eating, unperturbed. ↷

The robins have an advantage over the cats: they see the whole scene—trees, house, air, snow, cats, apples, birds, in all directions—all at once. For them, there is only the flock. The individual robin itself—the bird that sees—is the only point of absence in the world: it is the other robins that are present.

This kind of Stalinist social organization drives the predatory cats wild, for they are obsessed with presence, with strong borders mapped between the self and everything else. They are the great, Romantic individualists. Angst they know, but they are singularly uncluttered by fate. Despite this freedom, though, they have to swallow their pride and be relentlessly observed, from ninety points at once. They put up with it, because this is the first thing that has been happening since the first stars of snow fell in October and the world hushed and went still, five months ago. They persist in it, their tails thrashing with frustration.

The feeding continues until all light has drained away, and commences again the next day at dawn when the birds drift in singly, puffed up with cold. By late afternoon, when the snow is melting again and the river is again flowing down the driveway, the garden is littered with brown shreds of apples, like starlight frozen as it spattered over the earth. At the centre of each splash of brown apple pulp is the skin of an apple laid completely flat and pecked clean of all flesh: a jagged, mottled pattern of beak-punctures. The whole garden is like a canvas splattered with paint by Jackson Pollock in a New York studio to capture the essence of movement and the movement of thought. ☀

The male robins are the first to return. As far as anyone need know, they have come back to scout out and compete for territory—jostling shoulders, showing each other up like a bunch of teenage boys with unwashed socks playing LAN games in their garage for a weekend. Don't buy it. All that territorial preparation is just bolstering and bluster. They are really gearing themselves up for the arrival of the females in two weeks. When the females come with their hair dryers and their matching luggage, the males will be as tight as a hockey team on the eve of the Stanley Cup. They will have their world whipped into shape. They will have settled what they needed to settle and will be ready to ease down into family routine.

Well, that's the way it looks. In reality, they're having a big party in the corporate suite. That's the way life is with male robins: a near-complete lack of seriousness. They take life one day at a time. Hell, they take it a half hour at a time. For them, this kind of rootless life is not a problem, at all. For other birds, red-winged blackbirds for instance, territory may be important, down to the last willow bush struggling out of thistles and the last scrubby saskatoon blasted with tent caterpillars, but for robins, territory is a flux. If you want Boardwalk, they'll trade it to you for Baltic Avenue and Short Line Railroad. Life is not a war game for them, whereas a blackbird's head is full of operational charts and troop deployments. At their parties, robins are not staying up all night dreaming of world conquest; they're not even playing Risk, with their two-litre bottles of Coke, their chips, and their dill pickle dip and bad jokes and groans and farts and taunts. It's just a flux. It's not a mystery.

After the big, two-week bachelor bash in my garden, the females come. By then, the ground is no longer frozen and it's possible to get a decent meal of worms. The robins slurp them down like spaghetti. The males don't have to nearly freeze to death every night in the trees anymore. They leave their buddies, each pick up a powder-blue suitcase, and split up with the females in great good humour—almost as if cheering each other on with nudges and winks. Even when there are territorial disputes later, with males trying to cut in on other females, it feels as if this party, in a society with no restraints on behaviour, with no moral code whatsoever, is still going on. If we tried to party that hard, it would kill us at once. ✦

Every soirée must come to an end, however. Bruno showed me that. Bruno is a robin that materialized with the other males this spring but hung around long after all the others had paired up and gone their separate ways in the forest—finding a dark corner after the prom, so to speak. Bruno spent hours sitting on the gravel at the edge of the driveway, with the now-dry river channel running past his feet, staring at the shells of apples we laid out there for him: apples of pity. Bruno had liver spots on his beak, his eyes were glazed over with cataracts, and his feathers were a mess. He looked like an old man rummaging around in the dumpsters and alleys of East Vancouver, dressed in crumpled, stained polyester pants two sizes too large, pulled up tightly with a belt around his waist, shuffling, hopped up on vanilla extract when what he really needed was a bottle of Grecian Formula. He was still bright of spirit, though, as if he had gone transparent, as if the next life was already shining through him.

The most Bruno could manage of a flight up into the aspens or a swoop across the road into the firs past the meadow would be a short hop a couple yards up into a low branch. It would sway beneath him like a snake. Bruno looked as if he had had a stroke. It was a wonder the cats did not get him. Maybe they did, because after a week Bruno was gone. The last pale glimmer of colour on his grey and mottled Salvation Army breast was no longer there. His drinking friends were all off, doing the old trick, tapping their fingers on the ground in imitation of rain to scare the worms to the surface, so they could feed their kids. They didn't even hold a wake. ⇥

I started throwing apples out for the robins ten years ago. It was a cold spring that year, after a long, snowy winter of owls hunting along the lake at night and low, heavy skies during the day. The snow hung on through late March, crusted and hard. When it had first fallen, almost daily from November through January, and even later in the long, grey storms of the full moon in late February, it had come down in big starry flakes, each with the veins of a leaf—without the leaf. By late March the snow was freeze-dried, like Folger's Instant Coffee: thawed, evaporated into the dry air, refrozen, fallen into itself, drenched with freezing rain. It was no longer made out of flakes, but out of small, round balls of clear ice. It shone in an unreal blue across the landscape.

On the Plateau in March we call that colour white. There are no Pantone Colour Process charts here to standardize colour, like those little red and yellow and blue and black squares in the margin of the Weekend Edition of the *Vancouver Sun*. Colour is more relative than that here. Whiteness, for example, goes through an incredible shift during the progress of a Plateau winter. When winter opens, like a Christmas card envelope you slit with a finger in your car outside of the post office, white is the colour of pressed linen and cotton, while at winter's close you might think you are looking at percale sheets and floral slips, but you're really looking at water, a blue substance refracting the colour of the sky at your feet and on the hills in front of you. Nothing is steady on this earth. ✦

*I*nto the cold and glacial world of March snow, the robins tumbled in one deceptively sunny afternoon. They showed up here out of nowhere because the only place for kilometres in any direction where they could get even the chance of a bite to eat was in the patch of lawn above Bob's bubbling septic tank. That septic tank was straight out of a medieval etching of Hell, what with the demons' heads being born as the demons defecated, demons eating their own arms and legs, and red-tailed devils in Hallowe'en costumes stuffing humans down big cracks in the earth with pitchforks. You don't get the smell in a picture like that, although you do get the picture. The smell is another thing entirely. And it's true that Hell is a warm place. The grass there on Bob's Hell was tall and lush, happily growing into the frozen air, although the rest of the Plateau, from Clinton to Quesnel, was completely covered in pale blue snow, like little balls of decorative soaps in a Portmeirion dish decorated with flowers. That Hell of a septic tank was like a greenhouse in reverse. It was such a bright green it was like a UFO landing site etched across a high Andean plain. What with the smell and that big green runway light, no robin could miss it.

And they didn't. Every robin on the north side of the lake was there when I looked out on that fateful grey morning. The place was crawling with them. They were busily working over the lawn, break-dancing, bee-bopping, hop-hipping in imitation of the sound of pattering rain, drumming at the spring ground, luring earthworms to the surface so they could spear them, like Gitskan fishermen where the Bulkley River is channelled white and boiling through a wedge of rock at Mauricetown. What self-respecting worm would crawl around through that waterlogged and steaming ground, I didn't know, but it sure didn't look like the robins were having much success with their hunter–gatherer schtick. ⇗

I wasn't used to Cariboo springs yet. Standing on my deck, looking down over the robins, with the cat twitching his tail on the rail beside me, I thought that the birds had made a miscalculation. I thought that two days of warm yellow sun had lured them to the Plateau too early. I no longer believe that. Now I know that the robins do this every spring. Every March, they come to the high country several weeks before the snow melts and easily two weeks before there is anything for them to eat—an example of the kind of planning peculiar to robins. It's like the remittance men, the second sons of landed English families, sent with a pocketful of bank notes to the Okanagan in the 1890s to make their fortunes. Those young men rode up and down the lake on sternwheelers, hopping off at every landing to see if anyone had caught a deer, or if there was a chance of a party. There usually was. Enthusiasm beats out planning any day. The robins frolicked.

They spent the next day squatting in the branches of the aspens, their feathers puffed out to insulate themselves from the cold. Each one of them looked like he was wearing a down-filled sleeping bag, or as if he had stuffed a ratty old sweater with newspaper to keep warm. And that's hard to do while you're clutching a tree branch. The wind is liable to knock you silly. You develop tremendous muscles in the knees. Up there on those branches, the robins looked terribly miserable that day, as if they had been sleeping in cardboard boxes under Vancouver's Burrard Bridge. They stared out from the trees and over their own little green paradise, which had now completely reverted to winter, with no sign of a demon anywhere, except for a few blackwater geysers quietly burbling up. It was a complete reversal from the industry of the previous afternoon.

It would seem that the entire world of robins is racked by emotions as strong as Tang crystals on a child's tongue. Robins live for the moment. And that's only one moment. We, on the other hand, are hard-wired to look forward in time, even to times that will never be, and are proud that we can balance our desires with our realities and our dreams. The remittance men partied for ten years, some of them for longer. They rode the sternwheelers up and down Okanagan Lake, drinking scotch and gin, and getting off at the various landings—Okanagan Centre, Kelowna, Greata Ranch, Paradise Ranch—partied around a campfire, shot a few rattlesnakes, then caught the boat again. In the end, they weren't as irresolute as they first appeared, for they seized the first available opportunity to redeem themselves: in the summer of 1914 they stepped off the sternwheelers, and walked, or rode, out of the sagebrush, and volunteered for the British Expeditionary Force, and were mowed down by the machine guns of the German Army in Belgium and France. I took pity on the robins that day. I gave them something to eat. An army marches on its stomach. ⤜

In my early years in the Okanagan Valley, the spring orchards were littered with the scab-infested leaves of the previous fall. Perfectly preserved under the snow, exactly as they were when they had first fallen, the leaves turned black as soon as the snow melted and they were exposed to air. Their cell structures broken by frost, they followed every curve and indentation of the soil, rising and falling over every twig and blade of grass. Among them was a carpet of brown apples that had gone through the same transformation, bubbling and fermenting in the thin, yellow spring sun. The light came in low through the scattered branches, like a blowing fog.

The apples had come down in windstorms the fall before, or had fallen during picking. Often there were more apples on the ground than had ended up being packed and shipped. Golden and red, hidden all October and November by tall, mildewed grass, glowing, silvered with the tracks of slugs, the apples were laid bare when the snow melted away. The male robins came then and feasted under the trees. In those springs, half the robin population of the entire province of British Columbia stocked up on apples in the three thousand orchards of the Okanagan that stretched north from Osoyoos to Salmon Arm. In our orchard alone there were a thousand robins in the one acre of Spartan apples that always took the brunt of the fall winds. The atmosphere of that Spartan block was like that of an old-style beer parlour, with the blue, smoky air, the sawdust on the floor, the little, round, felt-covered tables soaked in beer, and the exaggerated, impossible stories. After three glasses of the pale, soapy draught served in places like that, with the foam slithering down the sides of the glasses, you'd make your way to the urinals in the back. They smelled like yeast. Someone would invariably remark that you don't buy beer; you rent it. For some reason having to do with defensiveness and vulnerability (and beer) everyone always laughed. You knew sin in a place like that. You knew that drinking was hazardous to your health. You knew you had to do it to have a place in the world. You revelled in it. It was a mind game worth playing. ❖

There was little difference in colour between the breasts of the robins and the rotten skin of the apples. There under the trees, as meadowlarks trilled in from the fenceposts along the border of the farms—as if they were the voice of the sun itself—the robins got themselves terrifically drunk. The meadowlarks didn't. Meadowlarks are dignified and wild. They want no part of our civilized life. Their calls are crisp and clear and played on a tin flute pulled out of a back pocket, and they cut across all of time. When a meadowlark calls, defining its territory as the grass sways around it in the musical shapes of the wind, we are not only inconsequential: we are simply not there. Meadowlarks live in a parallel time.

Robins don't. They're right here. ✢

When I looked out at the orchard on those windy March days, the ground appeared at first glance to be covered with rotten apples. The air was flooded with their acidic scent. On a second glance, though, as I held my gaze steady just a little longer, like one of those optical illusions in a book for children, with parallel lines appearing to converge, and swimming black dots, and elephants with five legs, the ground came alive in front of my eyes. What had seemed a moment before to be stillness was now a fluttering whirr of wings and the slow bobbing movements of robins. This is not to say, of course, that all the robins were either feasting or in movement. They certainly were not. Many of them were squatting drunkenly between the apples. Others were staggering along on their twig legs, scarcely able to balance on those stilts. They were definitely top heavy. Others fell over, crashing down like the giant when Jack got to work on his beanstalk with his axe. Some of the robins lay on the grass in thin pools of sunlight, feebly and determinedly lifting one wing from the ground and dropping it, with no force behind the movement, over and over again. This debauchery continued for two weeks every spring, until the females came. They fluttered in one afternoon, sifting through the branches of the elms, out of the sagebrush over the hill, and down through the purple twigs of the apple trees. Overnight, the males sobered up. By the next morning, the entire robin population broke up into nesting pairs and disappeared into the busy life of robins: doing the old worm trick, sitting on top of telephone poles in the evening and tooting their magical bell-call for rain.

There's nothing like the scent of rain falling down into the hot valley from the high country to get a robin stirred up—or to bring out the worms. I've tried it too, lying down in the lush green grass and drumming my fingers on the sod. Within five minutes, the worms came, long, stretched, and pink, like tongues spilling out of the earth. ⇗

On the Plateau, the robins still do-se-do and allemande. What's more, and seemingly impossibly in the face of their apparently pointless orgy of drunkenness and sheer bonhomie, by the time the females arrive the males have determined among themselves an equitable division of territory. Maybe it's like those old English families who used to run the Empire independently of the government by deciding over dinner that young Charles should get Ireland, and over an after dinner claret that cousin William would have to settle for Burma. They weren't all killed off at the Somme. These kinds of things still go on. There's no empire, but there is a commonwealth. It will do. I thought of Burma while I watched the robins huddle in the trees against the cold: a week before they had been in the Okanagan sun, drinking whiskey and water over a game of cricket. In pity, I threw apples out for them.

The apples landed with a thud onto my snow-covered potato patch. They glowed. The cats prowled in front of me, like hunting dogs on long leather leashes, tails twitching, bellies low to the ground, ears erect. Many of the apples were mushy, with a bloom of mould on their skins. The robins wasted no time at all and were soon busily slurping up the pulp from where it had splashed across the snow. To hell with Burma. This was a 7-Eleven, with a Slurpee machine in the back, like a one-armed bandit in a bar in small-town Nevada. ⇗

$\mathcal{T}$he apples have become a ritual for all of us now—and that includes the robins. Every fall I bring home five extra bushel boxes of apples from the Okanagan, and every spring the robins come early, in the grey weeks when there has been no new snow for a month. Within a few days the weather turns cold, the ground is once again as hard as iron, and the birds are huddling in the naked trees. That's when I practice my curve ball and my overhand, my slow pitch and my knuckleball, my bocce throw and my discus and my shotput. Sometimes there are so many apples in the air at one time it looks like I am juggling for tips, my cap set out on the ground in front of me. In that grey world, the colour of the apples spinning through the air seems impossible.

You can't blame the robins. God knows, there's very little else to do when you are a robin in the late winter. Why not get there early? The party circuit has run a little thin. One day you are on top of the world, the sun is shining and you have just made a big trip, sifting north through the forests, watching people's rototillers appear out of the snow, getting more excited every day. Then you arrive, the boredom of the trip is behind you, nothing can touch you, and the next day you are miserable and cold and wish you were a stone.

Every year I throw out apples for the robins, and every year more robins show up than did the year before. I'm on my tenth generation of robins now. I have my own little streetcorner in the robins' collective unconscious. Word is getting around. What a party. All the guests stay late, until I've run out of rotten apples and start dipping into my good ones to feed them. When I carry the glowing yellow apples out in a bucket there are a hundred birds pacing around on what is by then bare, black, and soggy soil glimmering in the sun. They all rise up into the trees when I start to throw the apples, except for a few brave ones, who stand in the shadow of the dogwoods, gargling and gulping down the sweet pulp. ⇗

$\mathcal{M}$y friend Rob, a tall, freckled, red-haired rock-climbing instructor, once stood in the main meeting hall of the Outward Bound Mountain Camp at Ashnola and told me that he had no respect at all for robins—that he had, in fact, no respect for any bird or creature that has managed to adapt so well to artificial human habitats. He wanted his world wild. Hey, he was young. So was I. I agreed with him. Around us, acid-smelling climbing clothes and sweatshirts were piled up amidst greasy sleeping bags, climbing skis and ropes, in front of the tall, shale fireplace of the camp's main hall—the largest of a series of A-frame huts set in a semi-circle above the old, washed-out Ashnola River bridge. Through the tall window opposite the fireplace, the cliffs of the Ashnola Valley opened up, dotted with the small, white clouds of mountain goats. There was a time not so long ago when those sure-footed goats—related to chamois, actually, not to goats—were on the must-see list of the European nobility. The nobility came, too, armed to the teeth. Even Archduke Franz Ferdinand of Austria came out from Europe for a bit of sport, before the world went all to hell.

It was February at Outward Bound. The river was reflecting a silver sky and the grey cottonwoods along its bank. "They're not real," Rob said, standing in front of his wall of glass, looking into the room, with the blue mountain climbing at his back, and high, high above it a thin crack of sky. I had come back to the Similkameen for a weekend to clear my head from university, where I was reading way too much Schopenhauer. It was making me positively depressed. I was reading way too much Nietzsche, too. For a young German kid like me, all that talk of the Will and overcoming the self was poison. You can't always live in your head. God knows, I tried, though, forcing myself to get no more than five hours of sleep a night so I'd have time to read a few more books. I got up to thirty a night—then I finally snapped. Exhausted, full to the brim with failure to climb that Tower of Babel of books, I had come home, and there in the late winter cold, with the Similkameen River spilling over green ice below the lodge, and an endless wind flowing out of the high country of the Ashnola, I laughed at Rob's joke, in the way young men laugh to cover over bewilderment. Up until that point, I had never thought about robins.

I have now. Back then, Rob and I were intent on discovering the earth itself, beyond our conceptions of what that earth might be, and were eager to move out into what we found. Back in the 1970s, when there was still an independent culture out on the land, it was still possible to dream like that about colonization, adventure, and the earth. We felt that if we could immerse ourselves in an earth freed of all human definitions, we would be able to discover ourselves, even to move into ourselves and be at ease. We would have an eternal knowledge, and that's a hell of a lot better than being a young man and not knowing how the world works. We were willing to spend a decade getting to that eternity. Against that purity of intent, robins, the great adapters, seemed to be betrayers. They seemed to be getting in the way. Which they were, of course. God knows, something had to. ✦

Rather than immersing myself, I drowned. When I came back up for air twenty years later, I was a different man. Now I believe that the robins are the ultimate survivors. These guys are able to adapt to any situation. The trick is simple: they live in the present, the moment that is always vanishing from under our feet. When you live in such an ungrounded reality, you are able to push aside the boundaries of your life, continuously. A robin, its emotions, and its perceptions are seamless. In robin experience, those three qualities are one, a conception so far from our patterns of perception that we have to give it three separate words, like the yellow, blue, and red films used to separate photographs into printable technology.

There is a lesson here for young men, and middle-aged ones as well: it is pretty hard to get angry at a robin. The coastal peoples of what in our tea chests of words we have come to call British Columbia refused to hunt robins, for robins were here on this earth only for their own sheer happiness, harming no-one, as if they were—and are—living a completely parallel existence on a completely parallel earth, joined to ours only through the window that is a robin. And through apples. And a good throwing arm. ⇝⇝⇝

The Blackbird Jug Band

A bird does not sing because it has an answer.
It sings because it has a song.
> ＊Chinese Proverb

Riding past the east end of the lake yesterday, I saw the red tufts of a grebe's head in a pool of open water no bigger than a child's plastic wading pool, and as I raked the grass on the lawn to pull up the old thatch this morning, I heard the skirr of a blackbird. Spring is coming with urgency, building up stronger and stronger as every hour passes. For the past few days, the chickadees have been passing through, small scurries of feathers in the bushes behind the shed. There is a faint tang of smoke on the air from the grass fires the ranchers are setting to clear their pastures and fencelines.

Last night was unseasonably cold—if unseasonable can be said of this climate. At three thousand feet altitude, snow is a certainty five months of the year, likely for six, and a passing craze for two more. Summer hailstorms often carpet the ground to a depth of two inches, and although the area shows up as Class 4 on the climate maps on the back of seed packages—with a different colour for each climactic zone—the designation is laughable. Thunderstorms even come in the middle of the winter, the hailstones bouncing off the frozen, melted, and refrozen crusts of snow. There is not much that survives winter here unless it is buried beneath the snow, and hard frosts can be counted

on from the end of September to the third week of May, although frost often also comes in the third week of August and the first week of June. You plant what you can here, and you take your chances.

Early this morning the cat brought several chickadees to the door. Others were scattered over the roads leading into town—frozen to death in the night. Those still alive are moving sluggishly through the bushes, easy prey for the cat, who slips through the scrub on well-travelled paths of his own making. He doesn't have a large territory, but he knows it intimately, so that if even a blade of grass is turned by a mouse flicking it with its tail while passing during the night he is drawn to it immediately— his mind a map of difference, not, like mine, of similarity.

I have locked the cat inside for the day.

The ground outside is frozen an inch down. My shovel just bounces against it. ⇗

After years watching the birds sparkle throughout the trees of the Plateau, flitter and flash, trill and boom from the reeds, flare and croak, lumber and dive, shiver like leaves in a rising storm, scatter light like birches in a mid-day sun, I have observed that each species of bird lives on a parallel earth. Some of them are worlds of pure blue light. Some of them are intricate contraptions of wood and grass, bound together with thought and aimed at the sun, to catch it and turn it into sound. These worlds bellow and hush. They sigh around Leandra and me as the wind catches the crowns of the trees and we walk, as tiny as shrews, on the forest trails among the Oregon grape and the soapberries. All of these many delicate, baroque, wild, and roaring worlds are far older than ours. We are the new kids on the block. With our mammalian squeak and roar, we are just learning the ropes. The birds have forgotten these beginnings. It's like what the Egyptians said to the Greeks, when Alexander invaded, in his rush for conquest. "You Greeks are such children," they said.

We're not that much different than birds, though. We touch and sing with our fingers and the whole length of our sinuous bodies, just like they do. It's just that birds don't collect Depression Glass. They don't line their houses with Nintendo Games and Archie Comics. They don't fill out credit card applications promising an introductory rate of 3.9 per cent, which reverts to 19.9 per cent after three months. For a bird, there is no body and no mind; there is only the bird and the planet, spinning among the stars, heaving through the seasons—snow sifting through the trees, the sun drifting as rain over the slopes. We can see it, because it's not foreign to us: we step out of the house on a winter evening, and the green sky floods over us like a lake and we walk out, chill, onto the lakebed, and feel as large as the universe.

We have a word for this kind of existence that bridges our political and social intrigues with what we see and touch, hear and taste and smell: spirit.

No wonder angels are painted with wings. No wonder air and sky blow through world religions like light through a stone doorway: if we could ever introduce the concept of words to birds, they would consider it spurious, something too reckless and poisoned to contemplate, such as the civic administration of a Nazi Gauleiter would be to us. ⤳

We live on a blue planet spinning in space, with broad savannas and steppes, river deltas by the sea, cities, farmland, and the ocean breaking in surf on the shore. Of all the ways we could look at the world, that is the one we walk through.

The birds have their own worlds, too—from the high skies of the eagle, to the dense thickets of the evening grosbeaks, with their yellow eye-patches like zinc sunscreen, crossing the whole plateau by hopping in an unpredictable pattern in depth and width and height from branch to branch through the trembling aspens. These avian earths all live inside each other like the folded and infolded leaves inside a black bud casing in the winter, sheltered from the aurora and the nights of piercing cold that freezes steel. Each is as vastly varied as are our vistas of the earth: the white beaches of the Bahamas with the cruise ships anchored offshore, the heat-blasted deserts of Afghanistan with the mountains like ruins of hope.

The robins, for example, live in the free love of an Oregon commune: you grab a bite to eat, you relish it, you sleep with who you want to sleep with, you take money from your relatives and give it away to your lovers and the friends of your lovers, history flows off of you like spring rain driving horizontally across the Plateau, and you feel no guilt. In contrast, the blackbirds, who arrive almost as early in the spring, don't care to think about communes. They vote for the Republican Party. They sent their sons to Vietnam and welcomed them home—when they came home—as heroes. They don't want to change the world. They live in Antelope, Oregon, and wear Korean-made plaid shirts. They have big belt buckles. They drive diesel trucks. They are generous and look after their own. They belong to the Elks and the Chamber of Commerce. Their wives drive the kids to hockey practice at 5:00 AM. →

The blackbirds come when the night snow turns to slush by mid-morning and to damp, old grass by noon. They come when I haven't even thought it might be spring. The first to arrive are the males. They spill in one morning, in a colourless light under a cover of thin, low cloud that all winter had been a liquid falling over the earth. On mornings like that, I walk through a vast space; nothing separates me from the farthest distances. The mountains thirty kilometres to the north, rising blue out of the black morning trees of the Plateau, or the river fifty kilometres to the west, curling green and cold over its sandbars, are as close as my fingertips. My breath freezes in front of me. The cold cuts through my jeans, and suddenly the blackbirds are there, as if they have stepped out of one of those hidden-animals games for children, where pheasants and foxes and bears are standing within the shapes of the trees and bushes and clouds and the game is to spot them. They were there all along, their dark outlines obscured by washes of paint, but now they are visible.

The spring light lies over the blackbirds, wet and cool. Their wing-patches are pale when they come, like the flanks of farm-bred salmon, like ice-cream advertisements left in a shop window all summer, like leaves that have lain under the snow since October. Day by day, as the light rises, the birds colour up, a little brighter every day. By the time the catkins on the willows break their wing-casings along the shore and the yellow pollen streams in a thin wind through the air, the wing-patches are a brilliant red, like the gills of trout in mountain water. By then, a ring of willow pollen floats around the base of each reed, rising and falling as the surface of the lake buckles and ripples with the wind. The blue heron glides in slowly behind a screen of trees, his blue-grey feathers the same colour as the water and the air. He seems like smoke, just on the edge of vanishing. He stands for hours in the shallows. I can only see him by knowing where he landed and froze his clattering motion—like a folded card table. Then I make out his stillness. ✢

All winter, the snow blows in a thin stream, six inches over the ice. The whole lake is in motion. In late February, tall, single reeds, twice their normal height, rise taller each day, pushed up through the two feet of clear ice by new shoots anchored in the soft clay and silt of the lake bottom. I know the blackbirds have arrived when I see the first one, on the tip of the willow by the lake, framed against those reeds. Perching up there, he looks out over white, green, and violet ice: ice full with light, ice rotten and half-rotten and splattered with pools of water and drifts of snow. The crumpled, golden manes of last year's thicker reeds mound up over the shallow water and the muskrat houses, each with a shadow of snow from the winter's drifts. Among the muskrat houses lie black mounds of compressed reed stalks—like scraps of retread tires shredded off transport trucks on the highway—which the muskrats have pushed out of their houses onto the ice during the long winter. It's a mess. Part of being a muskrat is to go on latrine duty. When the ice finally melts over the shallowest water, the muskrats sit on its crumbling lip, washing themselves. They are supremely happy.

The blackbirds look out over all of this, as they will for the rest of the spring and the early summer, when the water is blue and black and white and reflecting the sky. For the moment, though, a blackbird's posture on the willow is completely out of place: there is no lake before him, no blue catch of water, no spill of sky iridescent as the wings of a beetle, no whip of waves in storm, and no female nesting among the reeds, just a single blackbird. And then later in the morning another one, stationed twenty yards along, and another, and another, with pale wing-patches like sentries outside of Moscow in the winter of 1942, staring out over the milky ice.

The robins have gone their silly ways, and our world, which is the intersection of all worlds, fills with blackbirds. They flash onto the inky, sodden earth of the garden, pecking for weed seeds. They flock and scatter like leaves driven by the wind—in still air. It is unnerving. There you are in the complete stillness, and you catch in them the edge of another world, torn by storm. They tumble over and over and flit and flutter and rise up. They sing. Most of all they sing. In fact, in March and April the blackbirds have a song in every slot on the hit-parade chart. There is no escaping their songs. They pre-empt the news. You might as well forget about the sports report. And these are not single vocalists, like Frank Sinatra or Emmylou Harris, and not rock bands with a lead singer, a couple buddies on guitars, a bassist, a drummer, and lights and noise and dry ice, either. These are barbershop quartets, and quartets of quartets, and mass choirs, in the wind and sun and rain, in the stutter of lawnmowers, the starting of cars, the slamming of doors, and the barking of dogs.

Every morning at dawn, as the light lies like the ghost of evaporated grass among the reed-beds, the red-winged blackbirds leap up in small, black swarms, like gnats, their calls unheard through the thick yellow light. By midmorning the males float together into the lodgepole pines among the houses. Motionless among a tree's branches, clustered close to its trunk, each bird at right angles to the bird next to it, in a multi-story column of balance stretching fifty feet up through the central column of the tree, the blackbirds sing. They are perfectly placed. They have arranged themselves in a ladder of music, a physical representation of chords and chromatic scales and octaves. They look like something you'd see on a music teacher's wall, next to the posters of famous musicians dressed in black suits, looking artful and smiling as they cradle Yamaha trumpets and clarinets and violins. I'm positive that if I moved just one of those fifty birds even two inches up, down, right or left, the balance would be shattered and the chorus of birds would make no sound. Their beaks would open, their lungs would flow with wind, but the result would be silence rather than music. ⇥

If you can call it music, of course. Forget about this thing we have about birds making music. Blackbirds don't make music. They yell. They all stand completely still as the tree sways and pitches around them and the wind flows through the needles; and with knees clenched and wings folded, they yell their high warbling trill as loud as they can. The result is deafening. It continues for weeks. You can't hear yourself think and you can't hold a conversation. If you manage to have a thought, it is shattered into a hundred pieces before it can lead to a second one. You get nothing done. Day after day the birds stand there, clutching the branches, completely unmoving, while all the rest of the world is in motion. They are like ships—charmed coracles in the Irish Sea in bad weather, full of snakes going out and saints coming in. Even the leafless aspens, presenting scarcely any profile to the wind, sway and toss, bend and tremble, like charmed ropes. The blackbirds must get awful cramps.

By dusk the songs are done and the blackbirds are rising up and sinking down again in the reed-beds. The tall, flaming candle of the pine off the corner of my balcony is dark and silent in the absolutely airless sky. The shallow waves have hushed against the shore. ⇗

*I*t's not the only way of getting your point across. Crows, for instance, perch on the edge of dumpsters and garbage cans and tell bad jokes you really shouldn't be repeating in company. To make its scratchy call, a crow channels all the energy of its entire self, maybe of its entire world, maybe of many different worlds, and any other shiny baubles it can find, too. The *caw* of a crow is a sound made by children in kindergarten. It's what we think crows do. The crows don't know how to make it. What the crows do instead is a scrape of twigs, a laugh and a challenge, which starts at the crow's tail, as far back in a crow as it is possible to stretch a rubber band, and is thrown forward, picking up speed, until the crow almost gags. At that point, the crow throws its whole body towards its head, its beak springs open as if it had been hooked up with a mechanical latch, and the sound hurls forth, surprisingly broken up for all that effort, and falls at the crow's feet, in ruins. Crows are like the Three Stooges, and laugh at each other for the sorriness of it all. In a perverse way, they are proud. They should be. The crow is like the funnelled speaker on an old hand-turned gramophone tarnished with age. →

While we live in the tension between trade agreements with China, the history of the spread of corporate life around the globe, and our own individual lives, blackbirds live in the flock. They might be yelling at each other in a pine tree that looks like it has walked straight out of the first age of the world, a feathered creature older than the dinosaurs, looking for all the world as if it carries with it much of the wisdom of its long journey, sure, but the next moment the blackbirds are all fluttering out of the needles, wheeling over the grey-green branchtips of the aspens. The tightly folded, golden bud-shells glint dully as they reflect the slow, white clouds. The birds flash over them, trailing thin, sooty shadows that are scarcely shadows, and settle in another pine tree a hundred yards along the shore, where they start the whole process up all over again. What a racket.

The chorus of the blackbirds is definitely not a song. It is a lot more like the sound of a factory, choreographed by a mad genius in a green velvet jacket cut from a curtain in 1914 London. Comparisons fall short. It has been compared to the sound of an orchestra tuning up. It's not that exactly, and it's not the sound of a bicycle bell, either. It's a shattering sound of glass, pipes, flutes, steam whistles pumped through a pipe in which is mounted a ball bearing that opens and closes the air passage continually, glass breaking, bicycle bells, ice shattering against the reeds in October, and the sound of thin leaves of shale chiming against each other on a rockfall buried deep in an arroyo in the mountains where the heat blows over you like a blast furnace. The blackbirds make all these noises at once. They might be in a group, but they do not sing as a group. It's not as if each blackbird picks up a different instrument and fiddles with it and tries to get some noise out of it and they all give up and start to pound on the keys and laugh, either. It's as if the sound is coming out of the air, out of the molecules of the world, vibrating in a last echo of the Big Bang when the world that wasn't first was. It's the kind of echo that permeates everything.

"So long!" cries God, vanishing inside his creation, like a jack-in-the-box wound back down into its little fairground. It's like the sound bouncing through the walls of a box canyon crowned with ponderosa pines in a 1950s Western: for everafter creation echoes with "Long! Long! Long!" and everyone thinks God is giving a message about infinity and the endlessness of God's time. Not so. As the birds know, God's time is short. You only get to listen once.

The early bird gets the worm. →

The songfest continues right through Easter, with daily small-group and sectional workshops, and lunchtime brown bag concerts. Everywhere there is light, tinged with papaya. God has been tweaking the hue and colour balance settings in Photoshop. The grass glows a little more brightly, the red streaks of lichen on the trunks of the poplars shift almost imperceptibly towards the orange range of the spectrum, and the air has substance, like honey. The lake has been collecting the light. It drinks it, embraces it, feeds on it. The two feet of winter ice has grown very thin and very soft and glows in shades of turquoise, bulging and pushing up above the flat of the lake. Some days it is a precious stone, set in a crater in the earth. On other days it is an eye watching, staring into a world larger than we can live. At Easter, the light of the sun glows right within the lake, brighter there than in the pale blue dome of the spring sky above. Those days, the sun is a pale disc behind thin cloud, of no more consequence than the moon on a cold winter's night—beautiful, but without radiance. It will not keep you warm. At Easter, the real sun lies within the earth. Its light escapes through the lake. It floods out among the trees and over the hills. I have often thought on those spring mornings that if I could only peel away the ground beneath me, if I could use my fingers to scrape off the mat of old leaves, or if I turned an old log over with my boot, the light would blaze out of the dark of the earth's broken skin. It's not possible, though: the ground is still frozen, and nothing will peel off. Only the lake glows: tantalizing, taunting. ✢

Neither winter nor spring, Easter is its own season on the Plateau. The last snow remains in ridges and eskers among the trees and in thin, scalloped lines on the wheatgrass hills. Long, dirty brown and violet rivers of cloud pour over the horizon, moving to the west at great speed. Tiny underneath these vast currents, the children are out on the frozen, copper-coloured lawn, hunting for chocolate eggs covered in bright foil. Some of the eggs are just empty shells of foil, perfectly shaped, with the chocolate lifted out with surgical precision by crows. Crows are very skilful with a beak and a clawed foot. They edge up sideways to an egg, pry it open, as if in the angles between claw and beak, knee and neck, they make themselves into can openers—mechanical dancers in perfect balance. Once they have pried out the chocolate, they move on, equally warily, to the next egg. They always have an eye on the house. When a knob turns, they know that a door is about to open, and they lift off in a flatter of soot the instant the first child steps outside and the door bangs. They sift away through the trees as the snap of the door splashes over them in slow waves. They don't leave in any great hurry, and they laugh back over their shoulders as they go.

The children find eggs in the crotches of the willows, in the deep cracks of the pine bark, amid the soft grasses and neon-green mosses at the trunks of the saskatoon bushes, and scattered over the taller, coarser mats of grass packed down by snow. All the time that the children are searching, squealing and giggling, the blackbirds are above them with their junkyard band, giving it their all and then some. They play and screech and strum and sing and hammer and beat their drums so loudly that it is impossible to sit out on the steps in front of the house and talk, because the blackbirds drown out every word. Your lips move and you might be thinking, "Do you think they'll ever find that big chocolate bunny propped up on the toboggan by the shed?" All you find yourself speaking, though, is Blackbird. At Easter we find ourselves shouting to be heard. It is a riot. Instead of being angry, we find ourselves laughing in the contagious song of the birds.

All that tuning up for the previous two weeks has had its effect on the blackbirds as well, for their wing-patches shine like Christmas bulbs, as red as the steak you throw to a guard dog so you can make off unmolested with the family silver. The male with the most brilliantly coloured and largest patch, a flaming scarlet like sumac bushes on the shale talus high above a valley in the fall, perches at the top of the tree like a Mountie on patrol in the Chilkoot Pass in 1898 as the miners struggle over the border into their frostbite. All the other birds are arranged below him in chorus: la la la, strum strum strum. ✦

In mid-April, the red spectrum is firmly established again in the world and the first touches of green begin to enter the light. The needles on the firs shake off their India ink and begin to glow again. Finally, the female blackbirds arrive, dirty-grey and brown, looking like bundles of last fall's leaves tied together with raffia and tossing lightly in the wind. They are so dissimilar to the males they look like a different species. You'd think they must live in different worlds. Maybe they do. Maybe their two worlds dance with each other, cheek to cheek. The colour is the most obvious difference, of course, but their behaviour differs, too. The males are rowdy, swigging back pints of porter and playing rugby and singing in their barbershop quartets, but the females are silent; the males like to stand around like argillite carvings on Haida Gwaii, like the stone heads on Easter Island staring out to sea, like policemen posted on every streetcorner in Vancouver during a hockey riot, but the females can't keep still. Without uttering a sound, they move through the grass and over the soil of the garden in groups, like Okanagan farmwomen gathering potatoes into sacks. They disappear into the tall grass matted among the red canes of the wild roses as if passing through the wet spring light and into a hidden backstage. There they gossip and apply their makeup and giggle. You can learn to see them, of course, but it is a new kind of seeing. Colour and shape mean nothing for this kind of sight—that's good enough for watching the males with the old bent binoculars on your windowsill. You see the females only by their movement. Sections of the grass ripple and condense slightly ahead of where they were a moment before, as the birds dart forward. When we watch them we are looking at a film shown at thirty-seven frames a second, fast enough to blur the human mind and give the illusion of seamless movement, whereas the blackbirds filmed it at eight frames a second. We are completely missing large parts of the world. It's like listening to a symphony, listening for sound in an art form in which silence is as important as the sound. Music is not called the art of silence, though. We aren't wired for that. For us, silence is the still of a winter night at forty below. It is the deafness inside wood. The silence of music is different. It is ordered silence, set against sound—just like the silence of the females set against the males and their E-Street Band. ✢

Things move quickly in the spring. The world of the blackbirds supplants the world of the robins, and then itself passes quickly. By the time the female blackbirds arrive with their language of grass, the trunks of the aspens glow, pale and faintly sherbet green. The last scraps of snow are violet and the shadows are tinged with mustard; there is no whiteness left in the world. For a few days the females scatter up with the males into the trees and the trees continue to resound like tall, green cellos in an evening concert under the summer starlight. Within a few days, however, the wine is long since drunk, even the stale wine left in the glasses on the banquet tables has been tipped back, the dancers can't move another step, the concert closes, and the birds leave the trees and move down into the reedbeds and willows in the mossy ground along the shore. There the female blackbirds hide in the cold air amongst the grey-green lichens that line the north side of each twig.

Finally, there is light again, intense light, everywhere. It has been growing stronger day by day, rising up through the spectrum, building up within the lichens and the air, motionless—a vast reservoir being filled by a meltwater river draining out of the Rockies, the turbines slowly turning, powering us, powering the infernal machine of the blackbirds' song. And then the light is here again—although there is still no sun: diffused by cloud, the sunlight is cast over the plateau from all points of the air at once. The entire plateau is completely without shadow. We have become creatures of light. It is spring. ✢

When the starlings return, those green-and-black speckled Brits, those ex-pats with their Wensleydale and their Cheshire and their Sage Derby sharp on the tongue, with the green veins running through it like an unripe apple, with their Marmite and their Harris Tweed and the shreds of pipe tobacco in their pockets, when they tumble and strut and preen themselves, the easy camaraderie of the birds in the yard goes all to pot.

I've seen starlings on the old horseracing course in the centre of Northampton, England. It was early morning. A few old men were walking their dogs through the dew. Giant pigeons the size of footballs were blundering through the trees, cracking branches as they splashed through like moaning minnies going over the trenches in Flanders and throwing up a lot of mud. The starlings were pecking at the grass, as starlings will. Everyone else I met in Northampton wanted out. They were miserable. They hated life, and it's no bloody wonder: two hundred years of civic planning is enough to ruin any city. Add to that an industrial revolution and its twin sister, its darling in braids—a war—and history is a blow to the head. The starlings looked at home there.

Starlings are pretty birds, with bodies the colour of industrial-weight gear lube—the kind of slinky, late-night cabaret "take it off, baby!" stuff that goes into the transmissions of tractors and that smells like rotten dinosaurs—a shimmering green-black colour. You get a little bit of it on your jeans or on your fingers and the smell sticks with you for the whole day: a tiny smudge of T-Rex.

The prettiness is for show. Don't be sucked in by it. Here on the Plateau, the starlings muscle themselves onto the lawn, their shoulder pads bristling under their jerseys. In the first period, they send out their enforcers, who body-check the robins, or just scare them away by their presence. Within a few minutes the robins have vanished and the starlings swoop and spin across the ice on their own. It's too easy. The bulk of the starlings come next, surging across the grass in phalanxes like the Achaieans on the dusty fields before Troy—and they move quickly:

nothing edible is left behind that row of darting beaks. Starlings have the ability to eat at ten times the speed of other birds—especially the happy-go-lucky robins who savour each mouthful, letting the light bathe their heads as they lift their mouths to swallow. The suitors who were eating Odysseus out of house and home, that long wandering veteran who took a decade to return from the battles on the dry plain in front of Troy, were starlings. They sat around his tables, calling for food and wine. They lusted after his wife. So what if it was politics; it was good politics. Starlings, you see, are opportunists. They are the last straw. By the time they arrive, the yard is a mess of birds and I have gone through four boxes of apples. There will be no more apple pies, no apple sauce, no apple crisp with oatmeal and brown sugar, no apple pancakes bathed in syrup, the apples translucent and steaming. There will be no more sweet peels in the sink, no more of the knife curling around the core, no more shaved pieces turning to air on the tongue. Instead, I can be found in the mornings out on the buff-coloured grass of the lawn, standing amidst the last, granular clots of snow, trying to convince the starlings to go off and forage somewhere else. All around me as I stand there like a scarecrow come to life under a fairy godmother's spell, the yard is a whir of wings. The air and the earth blur. ⇒

When the starlings come, the ground is thawing. It is the third week of April and winter is in full retreat. This is a good thing for the robins, actually. The warming weather gives them an easy way out. Already disgusted with the bad behaviour of the starlings, they just leave the apples on the ground and go out looking for worms. They are very Christian birds. They've been to Sunday School in the church basement with the furnace and the pretty girls from Grade 10. They turn the other cheek.

They aren't very discriminate about their worm-search, mind you, but there you go, that's how it is with robins—no attention to detail. Not for them to article as a CGA and pull the strings on the CEO and run a business from behind the scenes like a puppeteer in Salzburg, dressed in black, with a black mask and black gloves, playing the *Magic Flute* with marionettes. The robins do their taxes out of a shoebox. Actually, they are kind of like the Polish cavalry in 1939, assaulting German tanks with with lances and sabres—dashing, but not very efficient. That the Poles had some success; that they actually surprised and massacred a German artillery company in five seconds, is remarkable. Hats off! Three cheers!

This morning I saw the robins scattered all around the yard and out in the saskatoon brush, foraging for worms. There they were, hopping on their splayed rose-twig toes across the mounds of old grass six inches above the snow and across the icy drifts in the shadows of the young pine trees. Everywhere I looked there were robins, and not one of them was getting a worm. Well, big surprise: the worms were still a foot down, under the frozen soil, down in the packed, dry subsoil, curled up in tiny pink balls, like knots of knitting wool, sleeping the winter away. Far above them the pine trees glowed with the new sap in their needles, radiant, knitting their roots. That's robins for you. ✴

*T*en years ago I planted wheat in the curl of land along my back fence, where scrub had grown over the hastily levelled fill left over from the construction of the house. As I tore out the thistles and wild roses, their thorns bit my hands through my leather gloves. I picked the thorns out for weeks, but I enjoyed the tense pull of the muscles across my shoulders and down my back and the ache as I lay in bed at night and the dreams came, dreams of rose bushes, dreams of pulling, pulling, pulling and never breaking free. I had the brilliant idea that a crop of wheat would get me in touch with my German ancestors and their dreams of land, dreams that have come to stick to me like burrs and wormwood in the cuffs of my jeans when I walk out over the hills while the cows and horses watch me from the grey trunks of the poplars as if from somewhere else in time—as if with a step among the trunks I would suddenly be with them there, ten thousand years in the past.

I felt like the Little Red Hen. I calculated that on my postage-stamp-sized field between the aspens and the saskatoons I would be able to grow enough wheat to thresh it in the fall, to grind it in my stone grinder, and to bake one loaf of bread. I'd been packing that grinder around for fifteen years—one of thousands of granite soybean grinders brought over from China during the building of the CN railroad in the Fraser Canyon. I had picked it up for two bucks at a garage sale in Keremeos, detritus from the 1970s, when going back to the land was the in-thing. It was time, I figured, to put it to use.

I was still young enough not to put a price of any kind on my time, and for that loaf of bread I was willing to do a lot of work. It would taste so sweet. I knew it. I just knew it in my bones. It would be my way of celebrating my move from the Similkameen floodplain and of finding a connection to the Plateau. It was also a good way of getting out into the yellow spring sun. I couldn't stand to be inside those days. The sun was flooding the yard like lemon juice. Whenever I walked out, it washed down over me. The feeling of being drenched was intense, yet I remained absolutely dry. The contrast was most disconcerting. It was like living in two universes at once, and feeling both of them, as if there were two of me, but only one mind thinking and seeing what they saw and felt and touched. ✦

I'd better come clean right from the start: I never got that loaf of bread. I dreamed about it. I saw it rising in my mind. I could smell it as I pulled it from the oven and sliced it, steaming, and buttered it, and all my ancestors, dispossessed from their gardens and hand looms by the Industrial Revolution, rose up in their tenements inside of me and clamoured for a taste or a smell—a whole chorus of voices.

I tried for two years. The first year, the blackbirds got the first two sowings and the mice the third. The second year the Grade 5 class at Mile 108 Elementary School got the whole lot to thresh as part of a history class and turned it into gravel. Alchemy was their ticket. I wound up with a bucket of rocks. I lugged it home. I tried to sift it out. I finally threw it back out into the yard for the birds.

In between, though, there were two years of digging and sowing, of wildflowers among the wheat stalks—chamomile, bachelor's buttons, clarkia, and poppies—two years of standing out in the dusk with a garden hose as the light fell around me like petals off a spring bough, two years of deep snow and the frozen earth, the stars overhead like the ceiling of a church. There were blisters and wild oats, lambs-quarters and shepherd's purse. There was birdweed and there were thistles. There was birdweed fluff and thistle fluff. There was mud. Couchgrass made a move in from the old pine stump. Between all of them, I had quite a journey getting to my point of breadlessness. But that's to look ahead, down the road of disillusionment. Those ancestors are back at the other end of the road, clacking their tongues and shaking their heads, at how poorly he turned out in the end, who had such promise. ✤

All this work to keep from actually baking a loaf of bread began during my first fall on the Plateau, and flowed through much of the following spring. For at least an hour every morning, I'd grab my shovel and dig rose bushes out by the roots—and they were hanging on to the earth as hard as they could, too, I'll tell you, digging their fingernails in and screaming as they tore away. The clay was so soaked by the spring thaw that ten-pound chunks of it stuck to the shovel. For the life of me, I could not bang them off. I had to scrape them off with my boot—and then they would stick to my boot. The handle of the shovel grew thick and slick with clay. I even got so disgusted one day that I made a sign out of scrap wood and pounded it into the edge of the yard before I went in for the afternoon: *Ypres, 5 km.* I set it out where Bob could see it when he surveyed the world from his deck.

All kidding aside, it was slow going. This was definitely a labour of love—or madness. Once I loosened the heavy sod, cut it into small, manageable pieces, and shook it clean, I had to grub down into the dark clay with my hands to pull out the long threads of wild rose roots. They pulled loose like old teeth, thickened and clotted with knobs of crown gall. Now, that at least wasn't a surprise. I knew crown gall from my tree nursery days in the Similkameen. I didn't want it here. Who would—a viral infection that gives the bushes what look like tiny, wooden brains on their stringy roots, brains that hang onto the thin, dark threads like condensations of thought, like strings of nerves. Well, brains, respect for intelligence wherever it is found, the mathematical sequence of the musical scale showing up again in the roots of the roses, or not, crown gall is highly contagious. It's the Hepatitis B of the rose family, and I didn't want it there, because as I dug I had started thinking that among the bristling heads of wheat I could plant apple trees, like Japanese soldiers rising out of an old haiku. They could be like ghosts walking among us. I'd plant them so that their blossoms would fall in my hair and the yard would be rich with perfume in the spring, and in the fall the birds could come in delight like leaves given life by a fairy's charm and would eat the small, red, frozen apples.

Unfortunately, as I knew from the freezing fall days when I was a boy, apples are particularly prone to crown gall. When I was a boy, crown gall was my own personal enemy. The water froze in sheets of ice an inch thick along the chill back side of the shed in those last days before freeze-up, when we'd dig all the nursery trees planted out in the open spaces in our young orchard and heel them into water-soaked sawdust. It was my job to cut off the crown galls with a pair of clippers. With my numb fingers I could hardly grasp the clippers, let alone squeeze them. My leather gloves were dripping with water, and on my pants the water had already turned to ice. We cut those bastards off to fool the men who would come in their rusty trucks to buy the trees in the spring. They didn't want crown gall either. Crown gall will stop your average apple tree in its tracks. It's like giving it two packs of cigarettes a day when it's eleven years old, in Grade 6. You could go to jail for something like that.

There in my back yard on the Plateau, with blue leaves of light and rain shivering on the tree of the sun, I was very careful about the crown gall. I was at it for two weeks. Finally, when every thread of root was thrown onto the burning pile and had gone up in blue smoke like an offering to Poseidon for safe passage across the drunken sea, I hoed and raked the new land and seeded it in wheat. It was like throwing grain out for chickens. Little did I know.

Now, when I say *wheat*, I am, in fact, exaggerating. It was only mostly wheat. I couldn't afford seed wheat—$80 a bag (special order down at 100 Mile Feeds), and settled for Chicken Feed at $6 instead. Sure, it said WHEAT on the bag, and it smelled like a silo, but it wasn't really wheat. Oh, there was wheat in it, but there were also oats, rye, and barley—especially the rye. And a few rocks. And some weed seeds. It was probably the scrapings off the silo floor in some small town south of Saskatoon. It was probably contaminated with smut. I guess in the general scheme of things the chickens wouldn't know the difference, or if they did would be unable to do anything about it anyway. When a chicken gets hungry, it doesn't read the food labels, pull out the carb-counting chart, and weigh the pros and cons between an extra peck or a quick trip down to the gym to work it off. On the plus side, though, it was so cheap I could afford to seed it thickly. I seeded it really thickly. ✦

That's when I discovered the other kind of blackbird. I hadn't even heard there was another kind of blackbird. Well, Brewers' blackbirds, yes, with their white eyes like the eyes of corpses. Those guys are good for decorating lilac bushes and alfalfa fields in the Okanagan. They keep to themselves. No, I mean a third kind of blackbird, one that does not keep to itself. Who would have known?

As soon as I had the wheat seeded, I watered it down with the hose, and as soon as my thumb was numb from the cold water and my boots were heavy again with mud—this time with golden wheat kernels embedded in it like Cheerios in a ball of peanut butter—the yellow-headed blackbirds came. With their golden heads like silk hoods slipped over the helmets of medieval knights, they are exotic birds. Their heads and shoulders are a gleaming yellow—not the yellow of sulphur or of dandelions, but of snapdragons and pansies, like splashes of paint in a spring garden. They had just arrived from a winter in California, and they looked it, in all their Lycra and their tans and the easy movements of the powerful and rich who want for nothing, who love their handcrafted granola and have their own personal psychic trainers.

Actually, I had seen my first yellow-headed blackbird a few days earlier, although I hadn't known what it was. It had been pecking seeds between the wireweed and clover in the gravel beside Highway 97. Behind it, cows lay on piles of manure in front of the old 105 Mile Ranch barn, and new calves lay on straw roughly scattered over the mud—not exactly aesthetically pleasing, but then ranching is not a delicate business.

Each spring the old barn turns into a birthing station, housing all the difficult birthing cases of the five hundred cows of the Monical ranch: fifteen thousand acres of grassland, soda lakes, and scrub forest. The care is rough. In the spring, the ruddy-backed Hereford cattle grazing on the spreading grassland pastures north of the barn look like wildebeest on the Serengeti. Clouds flare over the hills, and on the highway that winds along the hills big trucks on their way to Prince George and Alaska pour through like molten silver. The air they suck in behind themselves scatters up dust. It hurts your ears. It gets in your eyes. It clogs up your tear ducts. It's a hell of a place to stop.

Occasionally a cowboy rides across the highway from 105 Lake, where the lakeshore is stamped into steaming, oily mud by hundreds of cattle. A white-haired, small-headed Australian cattle dog trots at his heels. The cowboy waits there for the traffic to pass, and then slowly, in his foot-length riding coat, his sheepskin chaps, his silver belt, and his black, silver-studded hat, crosses the road, and slips in through the alkali-crusted gate of the farm as if the highway was not there and he was only waiting for a gust of wind to pass before crossing the trail in front of the barn, the marsh cinquefoil thistling up between the wagontracks, the blackbirds seething above the bulrushes.

And that's where I stopped. I pulled over as far as I could. I put on my four-way flashers. I left my pickup in the shadow of the barn and lifted two-year-old Leandra down. We went over to the rail fence to watch the newborn calves sleeping on the straw in their jackpine pen. Leandra loved them. I loved Leandra loving them. When we saw the bird, off in the wireweed thirty yards away, Leandra and I crouched down and watched it from its own level as it pecked in the gravel in the roar of the big trucks, its feathers ruffling and then settling back down as every truck passed. My eardrums surged in and out with the vacuum the trucks created around themselves. Trucks are big vacuum cleaners sucking their way through the land. They are also very egalitarian. Whatever they suck up, they spit right back again, all swirled and mixed up. They are like the flu virus coursing through the blood. I picked the grit out of my eyes. I was mesmerized by the bird. Leandra wanted to go home. ✈

$\mathcal{H}$alf an hour after I raked my wheat into the garden and the soil lay heavily over the dark kernels, the yellow-headed blackbirds were goose-stepping around on the mud. These guys make the starlings seem like gentlemen in frock coats, and that's not to say that the starlings are anything like gentlemen in frock coats.

Twice the size of the red-winged blackbirds and with years of practice behind them—long afternoons of whistling at pretty girls and making lewd cracks as they step off buses and hurry away—the yellow-headed blackbirds elbowed their way into the wheat feast. Within five minutes it was theirs. And they were good. They were able to locate each kernel where it lay buried in the dark ground, hidden from light. Those little buggers have X-ray vision. Clark Kent has nothing over those guys. There's a whole series of pulp comics based on their exploits. When they get around to making a movie of the series, they'll cast Arnold Schwarzenegger in the lead role—cloned. There'll be a hundred of him, dressed in black, yellow balaclavas pulled down over his hundred heads. Some terrorists had just fabricated a nuclear device from some black-market Russian plutonium smuggled out through Prague and Budapest. Arnold was the first line of defence. I wasn't thinking film scripts just then, though. I was thinking that the birds were a bunch of greedy SOBs taking advantage of my hospitality.

In a few days, I had to take it back, for there was a reason they ate so much: their women—in their lingo, their "little women"—were coming. They were a lot more Nordic than the female red-winged blackbirds, and they only waited two days. There was not going to be a party. No. When the females arrived, even more grey-brown and nondescript and even sleeker than the female red-winged blackbirds, the big, beefy, steroid-swollen males stopped eating. Jerks they might be, but they're chivalrous jerks. I think that's the thing about jerks. They probably wished they had muscle cars, like the twenty-year-old guys had when I went to school in Keremeos in 1974, pulling up at lunch hour, engines throbbing, and drawing the girls away from us like flies to flypaper. It wreaked havoc on our fantasies. The male yellow-headed blackbirds kind of fancy themselves like that. Time and again I'd find them in that wheat field without wheat, standing watch amid a crowd of females bobbing like waves on a brown sea. The yellow hoods glowed. They knew which side their bread was buttered on. So did I. The side that falls down. I reseeded the ground twice before the blackbirds left for their nests in the reedbeds. I bought a second sack of wheat. It had more rocks than the first. ✣

I scarcely saw the blackbirds for the rest of the summer. Occasionally I'd spot one among the shoreline reeds, a small rag torn from a bright yellow terry beach towel. I expected to smell the coconut oil. The rags swayed when the reeds swayed, bowed almost to the water beneath all that weight. Around them the reeds, which had started out the year as rich amber washed up after a storm on the Baltic, had become a living curtain, never still. Deer came down and brushed soundlessly through the thistles in the moonlight and drank from among the roots of the reeds. Sixty yards above the water the footprints of deer cut across the black earth of my garden, each print perfectly formed, as if the deer that had been standing in them had become air. The cats padded out at night and hunted muskrats. In the mornings they clawed at the door, soaked. I had to pick the waterlogged grass off and dry them off with a towel before I let them in.

As I worked outside in the strawberries in the following weeks, or dug up a new patch of lawn to plant currants and raspberries, I heard the yellow-headed blackbirds on the air. Their piercing calls came up from the lake, almost undimmed by distance. I could have sworn that they had come from inside me, something between a scrap of metal bending on an anvil and a squawk of surprise at finding your car towed away from a fifteen-minute parking zone after only seventeen minutes. ⇻⇻⇻

The War Over the Muskrat House

Listen to all, plucking a feather from every passing goose,
but follow no one absolutely.
    ↠Chinese Proverb

Geese are border guards between Hungary and Austria in 1973. Their heads are full of maps about who lives where, what stamp they need on their visas, the countries you'd rather they didn't live in, the countries you'd rather you didn't live in. There are just too many geese in the world. That's the root of it. They have to go a long way to find a decent place to nest. The ones without the right nerve or bluster to slip packages of black-market money under the table wind up on the edge of the soft shoulder along the highway or on a sandbar in a river that is bound any day to rise up and wash their eggs away. I know it's evolution in progress. I know, too, that some of these trailer-trash geese are going to make it with big families while their more enlightened and privileged cousins, with their university degrees and their BMWs, their Bre-X shares and their protected nests in a Ducks Unlimited reclamation project, are not. I also know that most of them won't. They are evolution's long shot. Watching it in practice hurts.

There is such pressure on good nesting sites that geese race each other every year to be the first to arrive. Snow, ice, nothing to eat for three weeks, it doesn't matter: the geese come and tough it out, so intent on staking out territory and setting up a rickety customs table that they don't

61

care that there is not yet any territory to stake. They start out by claiming the whole lake. It doesn't take long, though, before they're worn down to half the lake as the next couple arrives, and then to a smaller and smaller corner as more and more geese cruise in. Geese are masters at continually readjusting their expectations to the amount of energy they have on any particular day. On their starvation diet of the quarter-inch-tall new shoots of grass, that's not much. By any measurement, they shit most of it out again. It's a damned hard way to put on any weight. The grass is so slippery with goose shit, it's hard even to stand up straight.

The geese come in early March, beating the robins by a good two weeks. They touch down late afternoon in a break in the spring snow. When I say *break*, I mean it: it's snowing, a section of the sky about the size of a semi-trailer clears, and the geese come in like Flying Fortresses on a bombing run over Hamburg. One particularly persistent pair has chosen the north shore of our lake. These two are the kind of geese who wear matching leather jackets from his amateur bowling league: she sits close to him, in the centre seat of the pickup, and his driving is not exactly straight. They have been coming in for years now—a big gander and his more diminutive goose. He takes a 44 chest. He played football in high school. She's a size 6 petite. In all this time, all these years circling dizzily around and around early March like the TIDE car on a stock car track in Florida, they have never raised a gosling on the lake. That's a pretty impressive record.

What they lack in intelligence, though, these geese certainly make up in bravado and devotion. I mean, these are stupid geese, but they are endearing. They are pushing the envelope on stupid, but they're still family. Each February, I wait for them. I cross my fingers that this year they might get lucky: the water might not rise on the lake this year, the eagle might have got tangled in a trawler net at Squamish and not made it back for the spring gosling hors d'oeuvres, the dogs might not slip out of their yards and congregate in packs, swimming out in the shallow water and ripping up the goose nests and crushing all the eggs for the hell of it. The sun will shine. Maybe. ❧

The first time the geese came—my second spring on the Plateau—the lake ice was still a good six inches thick. It was like the deck of an aircraft carrier in the Antarctic, in a storm. The geese skidded wildly into the reed beds before they finally came to a (crumpled) stop. Oh, they started off in good form, with their webbed feet struck out in front of them like one of those water-skiers on Wood Lake north of Kelowna, where skiers train for the World Championships below the orchards and the subdivisions, making the short run around the lake over and over again, taking the plywood jumps at fifty kilometres per hour, right beside the highway—in their wet suits, with one hand tied behind their backs. Show-offs. The geese landed with the beauty and the balance of pure form. I saw the Olympics in their future. I was impressed.

Except: there was the ice. Now, a goose's body is about the size and weight of a big watermelon—with equal grace. With the inertia of their heavy bodies, and coming in at Mach speed, my geese wound up in a wobbling pile of feathers. Aw shucks, no matter. They quickly picked themselves up and strutted around as if they owned the place. And they did. There were no contenders in that storm. The muskrats were still huddling in the dark. The bears were still snoozing in the backcountry. The otters—well, no one knew where the otters were hiding out. The ice was unpredictable; even teenage boys kept their snowmobiles off it. There was just the wind blowing snow over the old ice.

By the look of the way the geese sauntered around purposefully, they had come so early because they had their eyes on the loon nest. It sat on top of a big, old muskrat house at the tip of the reedbeds, right before the lake dropped off into the depths and all that stared back at you when you looked into it over the side of a canoe was blackness— brooding. I rarely looked.

It was a mighty attractive muskrat house. Every day, the geese came back and strutted over to it. They climbed up it like Donald Duck and his nephews Huey, Duey, and Luey on the Matterhorn. They stood on the peak, a whole two-thirds of a yard above the lake, and surveyed creation. And what they saw was good. A week and a half later, when the water had melted around the edge of the ice, they had possession of it, and a title deed to all the open water in the lake. Even if that meant only a thin, dark ring of water around the edges of the ice, it was a sound investment: the suckers spawned there, yellow shadows in flares of mud, where the shallow water, heated by the sun in the glare of snow and ice, was warmer than it would be again until the middle of August. The first sounds of water were freed. They were effervescent on the air. Life was indeed good.

In between desperate hours searching for a little new grass sprouting out of the mud of the lakeside trail, the goose managed to scrape together an hour a day to sit up on the muskrat house, shaping its reeds to the curve of her butt by scrunching down and wiggling from side to side. Compared to the elegance of the loon perching up there, shy and sleek, laying her head down in line with her body so she was flat and she vanished into the stark spring shadows, the boldness and cheekiness of the goose, stretching up her goofy, white neck, looked pretty silly. It was as if Sophia Loren had not found her place in steamy Italian cinema, stepping out onto the set with a look of ravishment, but had got her first big break with the Marx Brothers. The goose felt she had arrived, though. Next thing, she'd have a house in Beverly Hills. Like any sequined Hollywood starlet, however, the goose's bliss did not last for long, because as soon as she got properly comfortable and had picked out most of the lumps from her nest, the loons arrived. And they had a prior tenancy agreement. With no landlord in sight, and no Residential Tenancy Act bound up with official seals in red wax, things got nasty. ✤

Loons have better timing than geese. Loons don't arrive when the lake is like a parking lot at the West Edmonton Mall in early January: hard, white, and—since the shoppers have already wrapped themselves in their empty wallets to keep warm—empty. In fact, loons have perfect timing. They look like they hit the G spot every time.

In truth, though, the loons are just as eager. They hurtle overhead daily, high and at great speed, like harrier jets over the Falklands as the sheep duck. The flimsy, thin, raked-back wings of loons will only get them airborne, and keep them there, at speed. They go so fast that it takes them a whole kilometre to make a turn. As they bank, the thin stream of air pours over them like snow over the windshield of a Volkswagen Beetle—up over the glass, hammering and hissing along the roof, then back down. As the air starts to catch at the tip of a wing, trees and lakes and the horizon wheel below. You almost expect to hear the supersonic boom as loons break the sound barrier. They steer with a single, cocked feather, one way or the other, like a kid with a joystick and a Nintendo PlayStation whiling away the whole Christmas holiday.

The rest of the time they spend at the nearest open water to the south. But they don't want to stay there. They're like long-distance truckers cooped up in yet another diner with aging waitresses and aging coffee and other truckers with greying beards and snoozing jokes. They just want to get home. Luckily, with these constant flybys, the loons are the first to know that the lake has melted. Only the muskrat beats them to it, finally able to get a little fresh air out of the gassy hell of a crummy house in which too many people have spent too many months too close together with old, stale food, no diapers, and a stopped-up toilet. The arrival of the loons is a cause for celebration. There is no surer sign that the world is renewed and will begin again. ⤳

The male loon arrives first, splashing through the air like a stunt man fired out of a cannon under the Big Top in Paris in 1913. He is wearing red goggles. He has a leather helmet pulled down tightly over his head. His narrow wings have hardly any sweep when he beats them. They look completely inadequate for the job of holding him up. He looks like he is totally out of control. He is definitely not one to make graceful curves over the lake, with a skilful fluttering and splaying of flight feathers on the wingtips giving pinpoint accuracy to his landings, as the bufflehead ducks do in the smaller soda lakes up in the hills. When surprised, loons don't sweep over the trees on the far side of the lake, either, or circle before they set down again, hardly rippling the water. A loon has to check his fuel gauge. He has to check the length of the runways, and whether the electronic homing beacons are in operation. For a loon, flight is not a business of curves. It is a straightforward thing. The only reason loons fly at such speed is that they are in almost total panic the whole time, just one wingbeat ahead of absolute disaster, much in the way a jet aircraft or a rocket is kept aloft by thrust alone.

Larger and stronger than the female, the male loon pulls into town first. It's out of a combination of sheer joy and anticipation, not because he's overly rude, or because he's an inattentive husband not willing to buy his wife even a bouquet of Colombian roses for Valentine's day, with their smell of ammonium nitrate and their impossibly green leaves, while he goes out and buys himself a new tablesaw and a router table. Not at all. That, and the bleak terror of just keeping himself from crashing into fir trees and haysheds along the way. He is like a bomber limping back to England from a raid on Cologne, with one stuttering engine and the navigator full of shrapnel in the dead of night.

When the loon hits the lake he makes no attempt at a graceful landing. Compared to him, the geese land like F-13s on the USS Enterprise in the Persian Gulf. With the loon, there's no goose body tipped back, no legs outthrust like a water-skier coming down from a plywood jump. The loon simply continues flying and beating his little toy wings until he hits the water, smashing into it like a meteorite. Water flies up three yards into the air, and the loon hurtles down underwater and splashes back up as the waves from his impact flare out in a circle around him, tossing up small bits of driftwood and chips of ice and the Styrofoam nibbled down to tiny white balls by the muskrats.

There's always Styrofoam when there are muskrats. Those poor little buggers are unable to leave that stuff alone at all. Give them a chunk of Styrofoam that's worked its way loose from under a dock, decayed a bit from too much sunlight, and they're like kids with pillowcases of Hallowe'en candy spread all over the living room floor. Presented with a scene like that, you have a choice: either ration it, two pieces a day, for two months, or you let them get it over with in two days, and deal with the sickness and the wrappers shoved under pillows and down the heat registers all at once. The loon shares that enthusiasm in his own way. Even before the waves from the meteorite have settled, he is bobbing on the water like John Glenn crawling out of a Mercury capsule in the South Pacific, drenched from head to tail and turning back to admire his trajectory. You can hear him whisper under his breath: *Wow! Cool. Way cool.* The whole area is covered with tiny pellets of Styrofoam. Some of them stick to his feathers. ✢

Four hours after splashdown, the female arrives—far more elegantly. She hardly makes a splash as she glides down and enters the water beside John Glenn, and bobs up. A few drops cling to her like pearls. Within moments, the two loons are swimming together, as if they never went down to that little B&B at the Coast for the winter to eat herring, swimming deep amid the kelp forests where the sun was a spray of light above them and filtered down below them into the deeps. In fact, on the moment when the loons came back that first time and the lake lit up with their calls of jubilation, it was as if the winter had never come. The loons spent the rest of the day diving under the lip of the ice that still covered the lake, swimming for a hundred yards out under it, hunting for fish. They returned five minutes later, bursting suddenly out of the blue water side by side. It wasn't long before they had their eye on their old nesting site, either. They too felt the pressure of time. There was trouble brewing. ✦

The conflict over the nesting site started one morning when the goose was sitting up there like a bad Hollywood caricature of Queen Elizabeth I on her throne, her face done up in white lead paint and her hair back-combed into a mess. That make-up was poison. Poison, though, was the price for being a queen. You wouldn't want to be seen in public without that mud-mask of lead, and lead powder in your hair. It must have sent her ovaries for a loop. No wonder she had Raleigh's head cut off. What did she care? She was mad. A cloak thrown over a puddle wasn't going to help that any. She had the muskrat house now. The loons cruised up to her through a channel in the reeds, and from a distance of twenty feet started to yell. Now, when a loon yells, it is a pretty amazing sound. The dinosaurs must have sounded something like that, puffing through the echo chambers in their heads like a symphony tuning up. The loons had learned from the masters. ✦

The loons had company that day. The water in the north bay of the lake had melted for about a yard out from the shore. One merganser was sleeping on the edge of the ice, white as a chunk of Styrofoam forgotten by the muskrats. Farther along the bay, there were actually the muskrats. The place was beginning to look like a small National Wildlife Federation puzzle you give to your kids at Christmas. One small black muskrat spent the day sunning on a chunk of Styrofoam, as if it was the tanning salon down at the hairdresser's in town, and chewing on it. Hey, it keeps the feet warm. It's great dental floss. The water is just too cold. ⇒

Mergansers look like loons, except they are white with red bills. They are the Santa Clauses of birds. They nest twenty feet up in hollow trees, booting their chicks out to tumble to the ground when they've hatched. From there, the little Barbies and Kens have to struggle down through the scrub to the water on their own. It's a good thing they don't weigh very much. They fall down like clumps of cottonwood fluff.

I know a goose that tried aerial nesting, too, for years. She lived above the rapids and grey gravel bars in the few kilometres of surviving river between Kootenay Lake and the drowned waters and underground ghost orchards of the Bonneville Power Station reservoir. A series of old power poles lined the channel, their wires slack, often broken and hanging down silver and black into the scrub. The old green, white, and blue glass insulators glinted dully in the foggy Kootenay sunlight, and some of the poles tilted over the water at crazy angles. The highway into Nelson cut past the top of the powerline on a bridge over the river, and for many years that one very determined goose built a nest up there at road level, fifty feet from the ground, in the middle of a sagging old osprey nest so heavy it was almost snapping off the crossbars of the power pole supporting it. The goose sat there for a month every spring, safe from all predators but ospreys, and, who knows, maybe she thought she was an osprey herself. What she did with her goslings when they hatched is another question altogether—tipped them out of the nest like a merganser no doubt and picked them up in the water (hopefully) or the rocks (more painfully) below.

Birds don't live forever. Eventually the goose did not come back. The osprey nest stood empty for years before the power line was torn down. Either her young didn't survive to carry on the tradition, or their mates knocked some sense into them when they were looking for nesting sites of their own. Too bad. That goose looked really regal sitting up there, while the traffic roared past kicking up dust off the bridge—she looked like she was really going somewhere.

Not like the geese around here. They're going nowhere fast. ⚹

At migration time—in May and again in August—the loon population swells on the lake. Instead of the normal two nesting pairs, there are up to a dozen. It always gives me the feeling that they've run themselves through a photocopier and glued themselves up to construction sites in downtown Vancouver, over and over again, to advertise a coming concert at the Vancouver East Cultural Centre. The loons meet in groups of four in the middle of the lake, swimming silently, black, blacker than black, riding the water like sealskin boats.

"Once," says Tom, a neighbour who has lived for twenty years on the second point down along the lake, "I saw a group of five loons beating their wings. They were moving forward in a semi-circle, from the open lake into our bay, driving the fish into the shallow water. As soon as they had them in the bay, they dove and ate them. It was very powerful." Tom is a very practical guy who speaks plainly, with a small grin out of the corner of his serious, set mouth.

Tom has been watching the loons, too. And it's not just Tom. As soon as the loons arrive, and as soon as they have their chick in the spring, and whenever the eagle surprises a young loon on the lake and dives for it, missing it by inches as it finally plunges into the water, or when the eagle does get a loonling, and the parents call out in lament across the water, all the phones along the lake start ringing. News travels fast. ✦

Every year on the day that the loons come back to us, every child living along the lake—and the younger the child the better—is outside calling. The little kids are damn good, too. Leandra learned to call to the loons before she learned to talk to me in sentences. At the age of two, her loon calls were perfect. I couldn't tell them from the loons'. Neither could the loons. When she called from the deck, staring into the blue fields of the lake through the white slats of the railing over the first green flush on the saskatoons and the wild geraniums, I came running out from the kitchen to see what the loons were up to. But it wasn't the loons. It was Leandra. The loons answered back. They wondered what was up, too.

During the next few days, I heard them answer other kids up and down the shore. It was like being at church.

The sermon didn't last long, however. Within a year Leandra's voice had hardened into human sounds and she lost the ability to speak in tongues. With every month that went by, with every increase in her ability to speak with us, with every word added to her word hoard, a little of her ability to speak with the loons disappeared, until it was gone completely. ✦

That day that the loons yelled at the goose, though, there was no mistaking that something serious was in the air. The loons were hollering at the goose. The goose, on *her* nest, was honking and yelling back. The gander was strangely absent, which was curious for that gander. Most of the time, he was as mean as a politician denied a photo op. Most ganders can get rather sour-tempered, but most of them also settle for a little honking and wing flapping, and that's it. When things come to push and shove, they retreat, sticking out their black tongues and hissing like the snake in *The Jungle Book*. Not that scary, really.

Not this goose. He terrorized the whole north side of the lake. My older daughter, Anassa, had already christened him "Hitler," because he did not have a broad and democratic vision for the use of the lake and was quite willing to follow up on his prejudices with force. He chased absolutely everybody who came near—except the loons. Ducks, dogs, muskrats, and even an eagle once, all received a piece of his mind, but he was absent that day that the loons came to kick the squatters out and take up their lease, legal papers in hand, while the blackbirds perched impassively on their twigs and reeds, taking the whole thing in like surveillance cameras at a bank filming a robbery from all angles. ⇥

The yelling went on for half an hour. After that amount of time, I expect everyone's throat was a little hoarse. The loons' throats were, anyway. They slipped away to hassle the fish, cool and slippery on a sore throat—like Zinc lozenges. I don't blame them. It was like singing the whole of *Aida* with the voice you usually use for snapping at the cat as it digs its claws into your knee, asking for affection.

The goose was pretty proud of her victory over the loons, but her hour was up, and she had to go shit and she had to go up to the muddy path and scrabble at the shoots of grass that she had already nibbled at in the morning and the afternoon before, in case they'd grown just a little bit during the yell. When darkness came, she and Hitler, with the prudence that comes with true cowardice, hid. For them, it was over, because in the last light the loons came back, on silent speed, U-boots slipping through Gibraltar on the surface on a night without a moon. In the pale, plum-coloured air, on the clouds of the water, they nosed up to the muskrat house and worked quietly at making it serviceable, pulling at a tuft of reeds here, laying some others flat there, building both a nesting surface and a water-level jetty. That's important for loons: as graceful as they are in water, their ability to walk on land is close to zero. For a loon, a good, foot-long hike from water to nest is the Boston Marathon. Every nesting loon runs several Ironman Marathons a day— and without the long training or the Gatorade either— just to lay one egg, on her own, without Lamaze classes, without deep breathing, while her husband is out fishing. ✦

Now that the pattern had been set, it continued for several days, although, thankfully, without the yelling. To keep everyone happy, in the end it came to a time-share. Hitler and Eva came in the mornings. Hitler sailed around the bay like a PT boat, chasing everyone away. Wagner was playing music from shore, with his sixty-piece orchestra dressed in black and red. As the day wore on, the loons bobbed up periodically in the dark water just in from the edge of the ice. Goosy Eva trailed around proudly behind Hitler. Once the bay was pacified, Eva sailed off on her own. A moment later she appeared at the nest, primped at it a little, tearing down the work of the loons, rearranged a reed here and there, then climbed up, as clumsy as a Victorian matron in corsets and bustle, and settled herself down proudly, staring straight east into the light, while Hitler patrolled the waters around her. In the afternoons, Hitler and Eva went to try to suck some more juice out of the grass, and the loons took over, gliding up silently, and spilling up out of the water like water itself given form.

Once the female was on the nest, the male loon slipped off and went fishing, and showered. He stood vertically on his legs, almost completely out of the water, and splashed the water up over himself. A rush of white water like angels' wings flowed down through his flight feathers. He lifted his head and splashed the water over his face, and lifted his black beak straight up and shook it off, and the water flowed back over his eyes and into the lake. All he was missing was a bar of Northern Spring soap on a rope. While he showered, the female lay low in the nest, so all I could see was her black back and the curl of her head pushed down deep into her shoulders. She looked like a shadow or a trick of light. You looked straight at her and you'd swear she wasn't there.

This was an equitable truce. It meant that for a while everyone who wanted to could stake out a claim to the muskrat house. I say "for a while." Like most ceasefires, it didn't last for long. The weather was growing warmer. It was getting easier and easier to mount a campaign. It was also getting closer and closer to the time to lay an egg. The border question definitely had to be settled.

The bay was still freezing over with a thin skin of ice every night, and the morning ice was often covered with a white dusting of snow. The snow looked like a lacy pattern of icing sugar on a chocolate torte in a fancy bakery shaded by plane trees in Baden Baden. That snow was so thin it vanished among the grasses at the shore, yet on the lake it shone out brightly. Despite the cold and the stars, though, despite the incredible distance still lying between the earth and the sun, the ice melted by mid-morning. By afternoon the water of the bay was blue and shining like a wolf's eye. By late afternoon, it was the flash of a trout turning in deep water. It was coming alive, in the same way a foetus passes through all the stages of evolution before becoming human.

By the next morning, the rim of ice had closed back up within three yards of the shore. Slowly over the day, however, the bay returned to life, and by mid-afternoon the ice had receded farther out into the lake than it had the previous day. Everyone could be a gypsy in a circus tent on days like that, with fingers full of rings and a crystal ball and a candle; everyone could read the future. Every day, more land was being reclaimed from the sea and added to the Harlenermeer. Pretty soon we'd be planting tulips and riding bicycles among the polders. ✈

The world was not just waiting for the pretty picture of the loons and the geese to resolve itself, however. The (so to speak) dry land was thawing out from winter as well. During the entire span of the truce, as the ice was rising and falling like the tide, snow was melting in the clearings around the lake and in the meadows and hills to the east. On all the hills around, water seeped through the mosses, trickled through the muskeg, flowed down through the grasses, and into the lake. Day by day, the lake level rose imperceptibly, but inexorably. Within a week, the loon docking bay was submerged. A week after that, the geese abandoned the whole development, right down to the windowboxes full of geraniums and the German shepherd in the front yard. We saw Hitler and Eva less and less frequently after that. Oh sure, they still popped by in the mornings for a cruise in the green water. I'd hear Hitler squawking and the loons crying out over the forests, and would rush to the window. Sure enough, there'd be a white trail of water across the lake. Hitler's legs would be pumping as he ran on the water. His wings would be flapping up spray, his neck outstretched, as he scared some poor goldeneye out of her wits, but it had lost its sense of urgency. It was just habit. He was just lashing out. His heart wasn't in it any longer.

It was just as well. That bay turned out to be incredibly busy that spring. You might as well try to raise your chicks at the corner of Yonge and Bloor in Toronto. You might as well try to settle down into a nest on Times Square in New York. You might as well have herded your goats through Leicester Square in London, the little brass bells tinkling around their necks as they munched on discarded theatre programs and fish and chip wrappers, and porn advertisements from the telephone booths, as try to play house there that spring. The whole reason for the kafuffle was that the otters had shown up. Otters are the RCMP. They are not birds. They don't have a sense of humour. ⟡

We first knew about the otters in the middle of January. Friends had come up from Vancouver to ski on our long alpine trails. Winter might be six months long on the Plateau, but the weather never cooperates for that kind of impromptu planning. Sure enough, the weekend turned warm, and the snow melted in torrents. Our friends were determined, though. The Plateau was definitely the right place for them. If you ever want a place to show your determination, this is it.

Slogging and sloshing over the trails up in the hills by Sucker Lake, or Succour Lake—no-one is really quite sure—our friends spotted otters bobsledding in the snow, floundering in it like porpoises diving and rising again in the bow-wake of a ship. The blood pounded in our friends' ears and their hearts boomed in their chests, loud, like crickets locked inside a thin cardboard box. They watched, enthralled. The otters swam effortlessly through the snow. They were made for this.

A month later, the otters had made it down the hills to 108 Lake. Cheering like the Jamaican bobsledding team at the Calgary Olympics, they burst down through the drifts and yellow ice of weedy Sucker Creek, the spawning channel that feeds the lake from the pastureland and treed hills above it to the northeast. When I first saw the otters, they were sliding and bumping across the pressure ridges and snowmobile ridges and old snowdrifts in a day of low cloud and no shadows. A month after that, they found the muskrat house.

They weren't the only ones, either. A group of eagles moved in at the same time. There were six of those guys, with their feathers that look like they have been carved out of old railway ties—five brown-headed, adolescent bald eagles and one bedraggled adult with a gleaming white toque. It was like a school outing with a chaperone, a rugby team at a flea-bitten motel in Prince George smelling of beer and cigarettes, with holes in the doors where someone had kicked them once—or twice in many cases—and cigarette burns in the carpets. I felt like I needed a whistle and a penalty box.

Now, don't get me wrong. In a way, it was just like any other day on the Plateau. To see a bunch of eagles hanging around on the ice is nothing unusual up here in the spring. With the suckers spawning in the shallow water between the ice and the shore, the eagle show is the hottest thing going for miles. Tickets are sold out to the birds long in advance. If a bird doesn't know some bird who knows some bird, she'll never get in. The result is that *people* don't usually pay it much notice. There are so many eagles on the Plateau they soon appear like crows do to people living in Victoria. Eagles are wallpaper. Still, decorator colours or not, it's more than a little odd to see six of them hunkering down in one spot like a group of leghorns behind their chicken wire. They even have stocky yellow legs like you'd expect to see poking out of a woven bamboo pot of vegetables at a dim sum in Chinatown in Victoria, served on a bed of cabbage and bean sprouts in a red-curtained room off an old opium alley.

This was not what I was used to. I was used to those high, screaming eagles of the Similkameen, who ride the thermals up the three thousand feet of the valley wall and crest over the fields of wild sunflowers at the top. As I stood there once, a golden eagle broke over the ridge right in front of me as I looked out over the valley, with hayfields pale with distance and an ocean of air at my feet. The eagle crested six feet over my head, hung there for a moment, then slowly passed above me like a pterodactyl. In its flight I suddenly felt the whole three thousand feet of vertical drop crest over me. I had to sit down for five minutes before my legs had any sense of balance back and had the strength to go on. I felt that I was floating on air.

Not on the Plateau, though. No. Eagles here don't go around with carabineers and pins and climbing ropes. They don't pack tiny Optimus stoves and pop iodine pills and strap on titanium climbing tools smuggled out of Soviet Russia. They are opportunists. They will pick away at any old, dead thing. The defining thing about the American National Bird in the Cariboo is that it has no pride. The poorest peasant farmer living in a cardboard box in a slum in Lagos, Nigeria, with only the memory of his cattle and his thorn trees behind him and his powerlessness and shame before him, has more pride than a Cariboo eagle. ⇝

The eagles stayed for five days. That is: they completely overstayed their welcome. But you know what they say about company up here: "They'll come once, and then you'll never see them again," and, "Happy to see them come. Happy to see them go."

Like a group of teenagers with their skateboards and baggy pants hanging around outside a 7-Eleven in Surrey, intimidating old men and women coming in to buy a newspaper and a quart of milk, the eagles lit upon the job of trying to eat the locals. This was a home invasion for all to see. It was ugly. And they were persistent. The whole lake should have been wrapped with yellow crime-scene ribbons. Police with loudspeakers should have been set up around the perimeter.

Scuba divers could have surfaced in the pool with a mobile phone and authorization to cut a deal, as long as all the hostages were let go. Instead, we watched it unfold. By *we* I mean myself, making chicken soup for Leandra behind the kitchen window, and the otters. Yes. By this time the otters had set up their beach towels on top of the muskrat house, and were getting a head start on their tans. It was, after all, the only open water for miles. Mazatlan. ✦

*A*t first the eagles made a few attempts at the ducks. There were about a dozen of those: a merganser, several goldeneyes, a pair of mallards quacking away, trying not to keep company with anyone else in the pool, the usual thing. Goldeneyes, wearing their black and white Venetian carnival outfits zipped up over their heads, are the favourite food of eagles. To an eagle, a goldeneye floating on the water looks like a KFC jumbo bucket, hot and steaming out of the deep-fat fryer. The eagles couldn't take it after a while. The smell coming from those buckets was just too good. One by one they lumbered up slowly from the ice, sluggishly wheeled over the aspens, beating their wings heavily, turned, and came in low, their outlines broken against the tangled branches behind them. This was a lot harder than couch potato time, sitting between the salal and the tide line down on a river bank at the Coast, eating rotting fish for the winter. The Superbowl only goes on for one Sunday afternoon, but the Squamish Bowl goes on for months. By the end of it, the eagles have lost all their muscle tone. They've put on weight. Their Speedo outfits no longer fit. It's not that eagles love excess. They don't. It's just that they fall into it easily, the way toast always lands peanut butter side down on the lino and comes up covered in cat hair. It never lands the other way around. Eagles never "do the right thing."

These eagles were definitely out of shape. Every time they tried their trick—lumbering away and slowly diving back like a sheet of plywood flying off the back of a pickup—the ducks saw them at the last moment and took off like hydroplanes at a high-power boat race on Lake Ontario, leaving long white trails behind them through the reflected high rises of Bay Street, then lifting off, narrow wings tight to their bodies. Those ducks could turn on a dime. The eagles didn't have a chance. They couldn't even turn on a quarter. They couldn't even turn on a twoonie. Whichever eagle was trying it for the day just gave up and plopped down on the ice to resume his Dim Sum impression among his fellows. Play poker with an eagle. He will lose for sure. ⬩

Man, those eagles were depressed. Eagles are prone to depression, but this about broke the lower limit on that. They got into such a blue funk I couldn't imagine them managing to claw their way out of it at all. They didn't move for hours. The crows fussed around behind them, trying to look busy, but even they gave up after a while and fell asleep standing up. Perhaps that's why the eagles stayed for so long. Maybe that's why they started taking so many unsafe risks. They just had nothing left to lose. If they didn't know how to fly, if they weren't sitting down on the ice in the bottom of the valley, they would have thrown themselves off a cliff. How in the hell do you commit suicide when you're an eagle? They haven't figured it out yet. Just the thought of it makes them depressed. The pharmacists of BC should get together and administer lithium to all the eagles in the province. The world would be a different place overnight. The buggers might even sing. Like chickadees. They might sit on telephone wires and coo like doves. It would be a sight. ⬩

After the ducks had proven themselves too elusive, the hungriest eagle made a go at the loons. He approached the problem with military precision—for two hours. He'd already burned himself out on the ducks. He knew what was in front of him. Damn, he was going to have no more of that. Marshalling what little strength he had left, he dispensed with the camouflage run over the trees and clattered up over the white expanse of the frozen lake instead, nonchalantly, as if he was just slipping into the store for a pack of cigarettes and a bottle of Coke Classic. He circled out a couple hundred yards and then made a short glide back to the open pool, as if it was all too much trouble after all. The pool was blue and gleamed against the white ice like an airport shining in the night. You could have seen it from Alpha Centauri.

Instead of landing, though, the eagle swung out a little wide at the last minute and made a grab for the loon with one leg as he floated by, like a pickpocket working a crowd at a stadium. The loon dove instantly, and the eagle flapped awkwardly and landed again on the ice—but barely. He tottered a bit on the lip of the ice, then folded his homemade flying apparatus and hunched down. Wings like that must be really difficult to use. Those suckers are three feet long each. Moving them must be like having two long, narrow sheets of plywood strapped to your arms and climbing a hilltop and seeing if you can fly by jumping off, with a crowd down below watching and filming it on an old hand-wound camera. Your death would be shown on silent movie screens across North America and watched by kids who'd paid their nickel and threw popcorn. They'd explode with laughter when you crashed. The crows were cawing in applause; but if you ask me, that applause sounded more than a little cynical. They were snickering and breaking out their packs of cigarettes.

A minute later, the applause was just starting to trail off. With impeccable timing, the loon surfaced, without rippling the water. He came up like Houdini a hundred feet away from the eagles, and swam slowly off further into the green water. Once again the eagle lumbered up, did his convenience-store dodge out over the open ice, circled back —and made another last minute grab for the loon. Once again the loon slipped down into the water. From down there he watched the eagle above beating his wings frantically, wheezing, and falling back among his skateboard buddies, all in a blur of light rippled by the tiny waves on the surface. "Ah, too bad," the eagle's buddies said. "Try again." And he did.

This time the approach was shorter. The loon was getting the hang of all this, though, and dove in plenty of time. Or so he thought. But the eagle wasn't through with him yet. Not this time. This time, he dispensed with the ruse of slipping into the shop to buy a bag of Spitz and some Gatorade. Well, actually, he just didn't have the energy for it anymore and he was out of change, so he flapped up from the ice and made a grab for the loon, just like that. In the world of eagles, this was lightning fast. For the loon, who had flown with Chuck Yeager, after all, it was like a slo-mo shot. He saw the whole thing coming almost before it began. When it was time for him to actually live the moment, it was already in instant replay.

Agitated and bored and annoyed with the whole game— simultaneously, by the looks of it—the loon didn't swim away underwater this time, but just bobbed back up again where he had started, expecting the eagle to have already collapsed on the ice, out of breath. The eagle wasn't as stupid as he looked, though. Or maybe he was. After all this practice, he had learned something—or maybe he hadn't: this time when the loon dove, the eagle hovered above the cool pool of water, waiting for the loon to pop up again. I watched terrified and helpless from the house, binoculars held to my eyes. ✈

The scene at the pool shone unnaturally brightly, wavering as the binoculars moved unsteadily. It was happening only inches in front of my face. The cold metal of the eyepieces dug into my eye sockets. I gripped the barrels tightly. This was before I got my new binoculars, when I still used the pair I had picked up at a garage sale in Keremeos for five bucks. They had the singular bad quality of producing amplification without binocular vision. Instead of two images, one from each lens, coming together to give a three-dimensional field of vision—where reeds stood noticeably forward from the water, for instance, a world made out of layers and planes of sight sliding past each other like the opening scenes of Walt Disney's *The Lion King*—it gave only two images. One was bright, the other pale. They were slightly offset from each other. If you looked through those binoculars you saw everything twice, as if you were looking at the world and its shadow cast on thought. So, that's how I watched it: twice.

My heart pounded in my chest. The water lay still and black beneath the eagle as he awkwardly flapped above it. His cohorts in crime stood impassively on the ice, staring forward at the scene. Decorum kept them from intervening. *If you're going to be in the gang, you gotta do your own crime.*

Suddenly, the loon materialized out of the water. I held my breath. He was so close I felt I could reach just in front of me and grab the eagle by the legs and drag him out of the way. Of course, there were two eagles. That was trickier. I'd have to make sure I grabbed the right one. Even as the silver cowl of water was slipping off the loon's black head as he rose into the light, the eagle dropped on him. Or, rather, two eagles dropped on two loons. I thought the loons were goners for sure, and I'd soon be watching two eagles, in their twisted-off-centre stereo, tear at two loons on the ice. Yuck. The loons and their shadows were just as quick as the eagles and their shadows, though. With scarcely time to gulp down a shallow breath, the loons dove again. Sensing victory, the eagles lunged for them still further, following them down into the water. ⤳

God, he was a hungry eagle. I wasn't worried about the loon anymore. Now I thought I'd be watching the dead wreck of an eagle floating around in the water for a day or two before his brothers dragged him out for dinner to the encouragement and snickers of their crow batmen who were waiting to carve cigarette holders and whistles out of his wingbones. This just didn't look like standard practice. Folks, don't try this at home. Read the manual.

The eagle thrust his cutlery set into the water after the loon, right up to his chest. It was like jumping off the end of the dock at the cottage without looking to see what kind of rocks are lurking down there.

Well, the cold water must have woken the eagle up, because he panicked then, which was about time. His big, brown, laminated wings were dipping into the water as he beat them; slowly and awkwardly, he struggled over to the ice and slumped back into his place in the gang. His chest was heaving. He should have known better.

An eagle is as limited as a loon, actually: fantastic in the high air, but almost a total cripple in a tight spot at low speed. And a complete liability in the water. With wings like that, it's not hard to imagine: trying to manoeuvre a body like that is a lot like trying to drive a Porsche Roadster down one of those rutted cattle roads south of Clinton, with the trees and the barbed wire hanging in from the side and the ruts about two feet deep, made by a 4 x 4 in the spring when the mud was running good. It almost can't be done. It's hell on the suspension. You're liable to take off your oil pan, and you will definitely lose a lot of paint. It's better to have a good map. It would have been a better idea to have stayed home. ⋄

When the loon surfaced five minutes later at the far end of the pool, he was breathing pretty heavily too. He rose out of the water slowly, like Venus ascending on the half-shell out of the Aegean foam, turned to face the eagles, and started to scream at them at the top of his lungs—a haunting, angry chanting sound that swept through the trees and echoed along the shore. The eagle never went for the loon again. Damn good thing. I mean, this was not only extremely dangerous, but it was in really bad taste, too. He should have been ashamed of himself. He should have gone back for nightschool classes, some upgrading, taken welding or something, anything, gone flipping burgers. →

Now that the loon had also proven himself more than a match for the hunting prowess of a bunch of skateboarding eagles with blond streaks in their hair and studs in their ears and brown toques pulled down low over their foreheads, the boarders turned their attention to the otters. In their sunscreen, with the coconut oil rubbed into their skins, with their shades and their bucket of cold drinks, the otters had watched the whole heavyweight bout nonchalantly from the top of the muskrat house. They lay up there on the roof like a bunch of models flown down from Toronto for a photo shoot in Jamaica, modelling this winter's swimsuits for the cruise set—nothing you'd want to swim in, of course, but they looked damn good—splashing in the turquoise water above the white sand, sipping cold daiquiris, never venturing into town. In town, the natives lived in peeling houses that were falling down around their ears and talk was of revolution. Going into town would be a definite mistake.

There was no escaping these bathing beauties on top of the muskrat house, though, and with the elimination of the loons from the menu, attention turned to them. At least the otters were on land. At least they weren't going to dive.

It was a stupid idea from the start. Otters are big. They don't look like it at first, since they move with such grace, but they are big. The eagle that went for them reverted to the first trick: sweep up over the water, curl back over the poplars to break his silhouette, then bank hard and come for them, wings tucked back like knives and forks slipped under a man's arms as he takes his place in a buffet table while the chef slices off the baron of beef. The eagle was almost fully committed to his dive when he realized that something was sickeningly wrong. The otters were looming up way, way too quickly in the heads-up display projected on his windshield. Those bastards were too big. As the eagle approached the languid beach of the muskrat house, where the otters were twined lovingly around each other, the male otter sprang up on his haunches, stared the eagle straight in his eyes, raised his fists, and calmly waited for a fight, hissing under his breath, "Come on. Try me. Make my day." The eagle continued plummeting downward. Up in the house, leaning over the white railing of the deck, I had a ringside seat.

I was sure I was going to see quite a fight this time. I put my money down on the otter.

Just as it had been with the fight with the loon, there were really two fights here, in off-key stereoscopic vision. I watched two eagles surge downward, converging on two otters.

I thought, "This is it. I am going to see an eagle get totally pulverized. In stereo. There is not going to be anything left of this eagle except for a bunch of chicken bones on the side of the plate and a little gravy and a crumpled napkin." I could see the crow batmen really laughing about that one, all the time feigning serious concern. This was one they could tell to their kids.

Once again the show didn't happen. Just before contact, the eagle lifted up. Instead of colliding with the otter at high speed and probably breaking his own feathery neck, he swept over the otters' heads and kept on over the lake, circling around to the west to eventually settle back in the gang. No one made a move or said a thing. He was damned lucky. What he didn't know was that as he shot by overhead the otter had lunged for him, and had almost caught one of his outstretched feet. This was definitely not a fast-food neighbourhood. This was like having a Big Mac bite back.

After the eagle had settled again on the ice, the three otters sat up together on the muskrat house, cleaning themselves and keeping an eye—or six, as I saw it through my glasses—on the eagles. That was the end of the action for the day. The eagles returned to their morose vigil, unflinching, unmoving, on the ice. The light died slowly and without shadows around them. At dusk they flew off to roost in the tall trees to the north of the lake and to stare into the darkness like a mirror. The crows slunk off into the dark to sleep and dream. For them it had been a great day. Break out a cold one! ✈

I expected more of the same action the next day, and made a point of getting a good seat, with an unobstructed view of the action but away from the direct sun, and far enough away from the pit not to get sprayed with the blood—all for nothing. The only event was one half-starved eagle tearing apart the muskrat house with his claws. The reeds stuck to his claws the way manure sticks to your pitchfork when you're trying to move a manure pile from behind the barn into your wheelbarrow, and then trying to pitch it from your wheelbarrow into your garden. A lot of it lands back over your face. It gets down your neck.

Poor bloody eagle. There he was, shaking at one foot, trying to get the reeds out of it so he could get down farther into the muskrat house. He had already been at it for an hour. It was slow work, too, like digging a ditch with a heavy power shovel and a couple guys with hard hats stopping traffic, and the big metal arm swinging over, positioning itself, reaching down in a roar of diesel and a stream of blue exhaust to scoop up one wheelbarrow load of dirt, swinging around slowly, and ever so slowly dumping, it and the dump truck receiving it on bent springs, creaking slightly. It was an exercise in pure physics. The eagle had to think through each movement, and those damned claws kept getting jammed shut, meant for locking onto a marmot and holding it while he flew back to his nest and his young, their feathers sticking out of their skin all spiked and sideways.

Maybe in a million years, the eagles will get this thing with the claws sorted out. Until then, it took my eagle an hour to get down through the muskrat house. There was a big pile of reeds all around him, fluffed up. I couldn't bear to watch, and checked in on him from time to time. After an hour, I found him feasting on a dead muskrat that had been inside the house, like one of those soup bones a dog will bury in the garden so it goes all soft and you can just suck the marrow out of it like marzipan truffle. You can feel it sting the fillings in your teeth, dissolve some of that mercury and that silver, but it tastes sooooooo gooooooood. ✦

The muskrat was dead because in the middle of January its house was just a tall, snow-covered mound, about a yard above lake level. Walking out onto the lake in those days was like going out with Scott onto the Antarctic polar cap. The snow blew over the ice in a carpet six inches above the ice, in continuous movement. Walking, you barely saw your feet, or saw them as if they were on late night black-and-white TV with bad reception, as a storm pounded the aerial on the roof. The flatness stretched forward into great distance. In all that white expanse, that desert that tore through your clothes and drained the heat from your body, the muskrat house was Mount Kilimanjaro, rising above the Kenyan plains.

It also made a great snowmobile jump. It was irresistible. That was the muskrat's downfall. He had built the tower of Babel, just one reed too high. If he'd skipped that last reed, he'd have had a decent burial, with all his family around, their faces twisted in grief. As it was, back then, in the cold, green-sky days of January when the sun seemed a distant rumour of itself and even its brightest rays sparkling off the snow had no substance, he didn't even know what had hit him. The kids on their snowmobiles just saw a good jump, and hit that mound at sixty kilometres per hour, their heavy machines rising up over it and coming down hard like tanks breaching the anti-tank ditches outside of Kiev in 1941. The muskrat in his foxhole underneath didn't stand a chance. The next time anyone saw him, one eagle had got something to eat at last. As is usual with eagles, it was completely without glamour. He left the wrappers lying on the street. ⤳

During the whole operation, the crows had busied themselves like the subalterns always milling around in the backgrounds of German military photographs from the Second World War—tall, thin, relaxed, chatting, maps in hand, their uniforms buttoned up tightly around their necks, looking up startled and a little quizzically at the camera. By the end, however, the crows grew annoyed with standing around, waiting for scraps that never came. During the whole operation, one or two crows had stood discretely a yard behind each eagle, like waiters and Maitre d' circling a table at a five-star restaurant. Now that it was over, they reported for work in the morning, spiralling and looping down out of the silver smoke of the aspens, cawing and yelling and whooping it up like the Nez Perce with their Appaloosa ponies and their war paint coming down out of Union Gap after John Wayne.

As soon as the crows landed, they started pecking the eagles, and kept it up until all the eagles flew away. The crows even followed them out over the lake, making stabs at the soft skin under their wings and jabbing them in their bellies and at their anuses and annoyingly plucking feathers out from the smalls of their backs, ouch!, and dropping them to see how slowly they fell. They fell slowly. It was the Bastille and The Leaning Tower of Pisa all at once. The eagles had had enough. They didn't come back. ✦

The crows did. In the blazing white of new snow covering the green and rotten ice of the lake a week before Easter, they stood out in the white tundra two hundred yards from shore. There were twenty-seven of them clustered in a tight group five yards long and two yards wide, like the Prime Minister and his bodyguards moving through a crowd in Calgary.

It's easy to see why a gathering of crows is called a murder. With their black monks' hoods pulled low over their heads, their hands slipped into the opposing sleeves of their robes, and their heads bowed, they passed each other in two rough, parallel lines. While the bulk of the crows stood still, some plotters and schemers and ne'er-do-wells broke off within the group and walked to the left, single file. Other grifters and pickpockets and fraud artists and political fund-raisers and bingo promoters broke off and walked to the right, single file. Apart from these silent, stoic, passing lines, eying themselves warily, there was an overall drift to the group that edged them farther and farther into the middle of the bay. Something was definitely up. Other crows flew in—some were accepted, some were driven away, according to no set of rules you might read on the back of a deck of poker cards: flush beats four-of-a-kind, three-of-a-kind beats full house, full house beats straight, spades beat hearts. If you want to play poker, don't play it with a crow.

Like all meetings of the Mob, no one wasted any time. After fifteen minutes the meeting broke up. Half the crows flew to the east, half to the west. It was spring at last, all right. The Plateau had been divided up for the year, like a meeting between factions of the Corleone family controlling various parts of New York, gathering for an annual conference in the back room of a wedding reception, with the wine flowing and big guys in black suits at the door.

Either that, or they were just gathering in an effort to break the ice. "Okay, guys. If we get enough of us to stand here, we can break this stuff. Okay, everybody, jump!" Maybe. ✧

Two days after the putsch by the crows, the ice did break. It split open in the big, sweeping bay on the north end of the lake. With the whole lake before them at last, the ducks and crows and otters and loons, the whole sad crew that had been hanging out on the sidewalk of the 7-Eleven pool in front of our house, dispersed. As soon as they were gone, a muskrat sat on the edge of the ice and washed his hands and face, slicking his hair back until it gleamed. Sweet peace. Sweet Lord in Heaven, thank you for your grace.

The next week was a time of cold nights and hoarfrost in the mornings. The morning trees and bushes fluffed out like silver birds. It was as if while we slept we had been transported to a performance of the Bolshoi Ballet. At the end of that week of Tchaikovsky morning, noon, and night, the whole lake was free. The North Wind swung around to the south, like a pony around its trainer in a ring of jackpine poles. Damp and weightless, it didn't fall down over us, but swept up and away. It was one of those winds that clean you out, as if over us and through us, always, invisible in the air, a Doukhobour woman is sweeping out the linoleum of a northern shack in the spring, and the broom moves right through us and we are swept clear, and we are lifted up and we are creatures of the air.

Within an hour of the first cool, wet breath of that wind, the pool in front of the house widened. By 9:00 AM, the wind had swung around on its lead and surged in from the east, grabbed a small lip of the ice at the eastern edge of the lake, and, using that as a wedge, drove the thin, grainy ice upon itself. The whole mess piled up three kilometres away against the west beach. It lay there on the half-frozen, grey sand in mounds two feet thick. From a distance, it looked like a crescent moon along the shore.

I walked out through the clear air, past yards packed with barking dogs, until I came to the moon in a wash of light. I walked through it. I kicked the moon up in front of my feet, and it sprayed up and splashed, like salt. I bent down and squeezed it in my hand and it dripped water. And still it shone. ⚹

For a few days after that, wind blew day and night. It roared and whistled and moaned as it teased around the outside of the house, looking for a way in. Branches snapped off the fir at the foot of my path and lay on the lake trail. I reckoned that a few more years of that and there was not going to be any fir tree left. The blackbirds were going to be pissed. I was missing it already myself. The aspens whipped and snaked and sang across the lower sky. Half the lake was clear of ice—blue; the other was ever changing—white in the mornings, green-black in the afternoons.

One morning, however, it was finally all over. Without warning, the lake swallowed the ice all in one gulp: chug-a-lug the whiskey sour, slam down the glass. Chunks of ice, clear in the water, were floating around the loons as they dove. As they swam down through that ice, it bumped up against them like the smoky cubes airbrushed in with the skulls and naked women they used to show in whiskey ads back in the early 1970s to get us hooked. We are surrounded by dreams and the unknown. Diving in that chill water, the loons had to navigate around those invisible squares. It was bitterly cold. Up on the surface, all that was left of the desert of ice that stretched, seemingly from my doorstep to the South Pole, was one ice floe, about twenty feet long, that drifted past in the wind.

For years, bored kids from out of town have been coming into Williams Lake to steal cars, whooping it up on the switchbacks down to the Fraser, then—as fast as they can through the bush—careening from ditch to ditch, torching the cars when they run out of gas, bumming a ride back into Williams Lake to catch another car on the street and make another go for it. The whole thing is a rodeo—a rodeo gone wrong. The crows floated past like that, as if their ice floe was a float in the Williams Lake Stampede Parade, built up on the chassis of a 1967 Fairlane. On this floe were all the neighbourhood crows, out for the last laugh of the season, just enjoying the ride on this last lick of ice as if it were a red lacquer surfboard, one of those things you could rent by the hundreds on the beaches of Penticton in 1965, while Elvis played at the Starlight Drive-In and our dad tried to get us to sneak in for free by getting us to hide in the trunk. We refused. The crows stood on their board with an exaggerated dignity, as if this was the sinking of the Titanic and they were going to wait it out, puffing on their tubas and french horns as the cold swallowed them up. I swear I saw them raise their wings and wave. ❖❖❖

The Eagles of Sepa Lake

No need to teach an eagle to fly.
　⟶Greek Proverb

On Sepa Lake, eagles are as common as pawns on a chessboard—at the beginning of the game, before the Queen weaves her webs of power, staring into her magic mirror, controlling the King with an icy glare, and all the time with her eye on Lancelot out there in the joust: mmmmm. The eagles of Sepa Lake aren't half so noble as all that. They don't have Turkish couches in their boudoirs and bottles of perfume on their cabinets. They're a dime a dozen. They're like those sport socks in the bags at Zellers, six to a pack, grey with white cuffs.

Sepa Lake is a small, leech-infested lake that joins 108 Lake by a dredged and reedy channel below the ninth hole of the 108 golf course. Late every spring, the girls and I canoe over and fetch last summer's golf balls out of the water with a long pole. After a half hour we have an ice cream bucket full of them: yellow Easter eggs dripping with slime. Everything on the bottom of the lake is dripping with slime.

It's not as if the balls are worth much around here, though: a bucket like that goes at a garage sale for about fifty cents. So much for living off the land. The eagles get about the same return for their investment, actually—which is why hunting and gathering has fallen out of favour around these parts. To put it bluntly, spring eagles on Sepa Lake are like Enron investors: there's a lot of hype and a lot of numb shock.

To set the scene: Sepa Lake is shallow, completely rimmed with reeds. It looks like a waving, blue bulls-eye in a green dartboard. God has been using it for target practice after a couple beers. The eagles are his darts. God's a pretty good shot. The problem when you're a dart, however, is what to do with your time after you've hit the bulls-eye. The eagles spend a lot of time wondering about that. Because they don't think quickly, they do the best they can: they think slowly. Watching an eagle think about God and darts and beer and the big question of what to do next is like watching concrete set.

Because Sepa Lake has little deep water to hold the summer sun, it melts early in the spring and freezes early in the fall. In fact, the first sign of fall snow is probably Sepa Lake beaming its white face up at the Crab Nebula—and God. A pair of loons makes its home there, forming the southern corner of the local Distant Early Warning Triangle.

Up in the Northwest Territories, the Canadian and American governments built radar stations during the Cold War so the terrible soviet bombers couldn't sneak over the caribou herds and bomb school kids in Duluth, Minnesota, before they got under their desks with their hands over their ears and their HB pencils falling out over their backs. It was serious stuff. Down here, it's serious, too—the loons get together to protect themselves against the eagles. Eagles are such cowards that the only protection you really need against them is the knowledge that they are there. Like a soccer mom in Richmond in her Freestar van with the Mary Kay seller's kit in the backseat telling her kids the rules about family passwords and watching out for strangers, your best defence is not to leave your kids alone. Up here, that means you don't leave them bobbing on top of the lake where they can be snatched up like picking up a bag with a Whopper and fries at the drive-in window at Burger King.

That's where the Distant Early Warning Triangle comes in. Any eagle that dares to show itself during the spring and summer is announced by the first loon pair to see him: the pair at the west end of the lake, the pair at the northern bay, or the pair on Sepa to the south. The eagle never comes unannounced. Like King Henry VIII, he has his own private trumpeters, belting out his arrival for all they're worth, the trumpets echoing brashly through all the rooms and passages of our lakeshore castle. These are the oldest birds of all, and they've seen it all. To them, evolution is a sad, sad story. They ride the middle of the lake like kayaks in Frobisher Bay. For them, it's still the deep Cretaceous. For them, it's like the Egyptians looking on with puzzlement as the Western World celebrated the second Millennium with computer angst: for them it was the sixth Millennium. They'd seen them come and go. Yawn. The loons are even older than the kings of Thebes, however. They move through the water like the condensation of their voices—voices spoken first in a younger earth and still echoing here among us, like out-takes from the sound track of *Jurassic Park*—except this is not *Jurassic Park*. This is real life. This is Berlin in early 1945. This is Kabul in late 2001. This is Baghdad—pick a decade. ❖

*A*s soon as the eagle appears over the lake, the loons raise the alarm. As their cries echo from one end of the lake to the other, they swim close together, raise their heads to where the eagle rides on his thermal in the sparkling white heights, and keep crying until he disappears. The other pairs of loons on Sepa Lake and 108 Lake pick up the sound and re-broadcast it, and within half a minute every other bird along the shore has made a dive for the reeds, the muskrats have slipped under the water like kids holding their breath to get their Red Cross swimming badges, and the eagle gets to soar high above the purity of creation, hungry as usual. Eagles are awfully hungry. ❖

But that's in the spring and summer. In the longest season of the year, the grey season between winter and spring, the season of felt and pressed pile and cotton wool, Sepa Lake belongs to the eagles. They hone in on the dead firs that rim the western reedbeds and hit the lake dead centre, much the way the Pacific Fleet uses the massive collection of posts and wires in a dry field amongst the cattle ranches and the coyotes at Riske Creek in the Eastern Chilcotin, five hours from salt water, to broadcast their signals across the curve of the planet to ships patrolling days from land out in the Pacific. The dead trees are important for the eagles. In fact, without dead trees, you don't get eagles. The preferred habitat of eagles is four cords of firewood stacked end to end, vertically. These guys should be in the circus. Give them a ball to balance while they're up there and they're hired. ⸎

Early in April, the stems of the reeds around the edge of Sepa Lake are little pipelines of heat thrusting down through the ice, fired by natural gas reserves deep underground. Warmed by all this ductwork, the lake is clear of ice for a foot around the shore. It is then that the big, yellow-striped suckers swim up from the cold deeps of the lake, with their mouths like evening purses that ladies take with them in their hands to the opera. The suckers have lain there all winter, barely moving, their minds tuned only to water and cold, breathing once a day in the mud. Now they are all a-tremble.

In cloudy winters in the Cariboo, the sun is a line of light in a complete ring around the horizon, lighting up the world from the edges like strip lighting in Ikea. Spring is like that for the Sepa Lake suckers. When the light pours in around the edges of the lake, they come up under the ice and to the edge of the ice and spawn in the yellow water drenched with light along the shore. There's some oxygen in the water, and they have a chance to breathe again. And it is then that the eagles come. They circle over and over in tighter and tighter circles, like a stack of 747s backed up at Los Angeles International Airport, waiting for permission to land and disgorge their packed rows of Canadians on their way to the wild van ride through the traffic to Disneyland.

The eagles are everywhere. They cluster in the middle of the lake. They perch in the old Douglas firs, two hundred feet tall and six feet through at the base, that tower above houses and barbecues and lawns covered with dog poop on the western shore of Sepa Lake and thunder in the wind like 747s taking off. On the open ice the eagles gather in groups. Sometimes there are two birds in a group, but mostly there are three or four. Always, they stare inwards to a central point exactly equidistant from each of them, and remain like that for hours, without moving so much as a wingfeather. When the slow intravenous drip of will finally reaches a critical level, however, they suddenly wheel up over the water, to either perch in a tree or fly off into the haze of the spring air.

Each eagle is always accompanied by a crow, which stands expectantly three feet behind it, waiting for scraps. The crows are not quite as patient as the eagles—occasionally they will get into a bit of a squabble, just out of boredom. In these squabbles, one crow will take a slash at another with its switchblade beak. The second crow will suck in its stomach and flutter sideways in a flash of wings, the black feathers grey with movement, sometimes, or sometimes moving so quickly they seem like a film from the '20s—with dead frames causing the movement to jerk across the screen. At other times, a crow will leap over the back of its attacker and effectively change places—or, and this might be a better way to put it—change eagles. It's like trading in a car for the latest model. It's like putting up your hockey card collection on eBay, and with the proceeds purchasing someone else's baseball card collection.

This puzzling behaviour continues for weeks, as the eagles feast on the sucker eggs and reach, stiff-necked, over the edge of the ice to eat the dead fish the ice fishermen threw there in the winter. ⇒

*I*ce fishing! Just imagine. It is minus thirty degrees Celsius. Your car won't start. Your footsteps on the snow are the sound of a fingernail scraped down a blackboard. You sit out in the middle of the lake on an overturned, five-gallon white-plastic transmission fluid bucket, staring into a hole of water in the ice, watching it freeze. The hole dances with colour as the wind drives the snow around your feet in a fine, white river as broad as the lake. You do it day after day. It is addictive, like *Macleans* magazine, like the editorials in the *Globe and Mail,* like any form of politics. In the spring, the eagles tear and snap at your discarded fish for days, visiting them again and again as yet more fish come free from the thawing ice and bang up again and again on the shore in the year's first weightless waves. ⇒

*W*ell, that's what people say. I've never actually seen an eagle eat anything at Sepa Lake, but the people who live behind their barbecue screens under the firs, poking their heads up to gaze out over the channel towards the golf course, tell me the eagles are eating sucker eggs. Well . . . maybe. What I've seen are eagles staring, for weeks. Monks are not so patient. But then, monks aren't so hungry, either. And they're not so cold. ⇒

*W*hen they take off again, the eagles fly a yard above the water, at great speed, the tips of their wings touching the surface like a quick brush from the lips—something you're not sure is quite there.

I thought they must be hunting something in this manner, perhaps hoping to surprise fish swimming in shoals close to the surface. I got my answer at Easter. At Easter that year, I was five hours south in Summerland, bottling wine with my friend Gord. As we siphoned the golden wine into tall, amber bottles, I asked Gord about it. Gord's a biologist. He'd know. The basement room of glass and subdued light bloomed with the scents of the wine, and our heads were light with the first taste of the new vintage. As Gord fitted the siphon tube into a new bottle, gravity slowly drew the wine out of the twelve-gallon carboy on the shelf above him. Against the clink of bottles as I steadily fit them into the corker, and the clunk as I drove the corks home, he nodded and said, "You'd be surprised at the number of different hunting strategies raptors can pick up."

His bottle full, he slipped the end of the siphon tube into the next. I slipped another cork into the machine and fitted another bottle in. "What were they hunting?"

Clunk.

"Oh, I doubt they were hunting anything. They do a lot of things like that. Physically, they're very smart."

Clunk. I fumbled for another cork in the bucket.

"Like what? What do you mean?"

Gord lifted the tube and slipped it into another bottle mouth. Unfortunately, the light was dim, as were our heads, too, and he stuck the tube into a bottle he'd already filled. Wine welled out of the bottle onto the floor.

"Damn," Gord said, slamming the siphon into another bottle.

"Not to worry. Occupational hazard. Remember how much of this stuff we spilled when we first started?"

Gord laughed and poured the extra wine from the bottle into a glass. "They do lots of really sophisticated aerodynamic things like that," he said, as I shifted bottles around with a series of clinks, like long-tubed bells. "It's really remarkable what they do."

Gord slid a tray of full bottles towards me with his foot. The wine hissed into the bottom of a new bottle. I still looked like I didn't get it.

Gord relented. "They catch their back draft off of the water. It gives them extra lift and helps them to fly without expending much energy. Normally, for an eagle to flap like that takes too much effort."

I slipped another cork in and pushed it home, and lifted the bottle away.

"Well, I'll be damned," I said.

Gord grinned. "Who would have thought it of an eagle?"

Damn. Not me.

Clunk. ✦

Spring doesn't wait for the eagles and the eagles don't get hung up on waiting for spring. They are not marking off the days on their fridge calendar with a big, black X. When you have no scruples, there are always other opportunities. Eagles are like heroin addicts in the Downtown East Side. They need harm reduction. They need a safe injection site.

Every eagle starts out in the spring as a member of the landed nobility before the Russian revolution, nibbling on caviar and lox. Those are just the hors d'oeuvres. The Real Meal Deal starts at calving time. Once calving is on in earnest, the Bolsheviks have just seized power and the eagles leave Sepa Lake, without wiping their chins—or tipping the crows. The crows clean up just the same, like black-robed women in Afghanistan under the Taliban, selling their old china piece by piece in the square, somehow making do.

By calving time, the pond just south of the Monical Ranch Barn at 105 Mile, where Leandra and I first found a yellow-headed blackbird, is full of meltwater. The old Cariboo Wagon Road, which threads north from the desert of Ashcroft to the subalpine gold fields at Barkerville, used to pass there. Teamsters used to pull the stagecoach up to the doors of the barn and change horses before squeaking and creaking on. To build Highway 97 through this country, crews of men covered from head to toe in tar, the inside of their heads burnt clean, simply laid asphalt over the old oxen tracks. Back in the 1860s, it was a convenient location for the barn. Now it's just too damn close. ⇻

For the Plateau, this is the Bahamas. Around the barn, the yard is full of eight-foot-high piles of manure. On top of the piles you'll often find a new calf sleeping, soaking up the early spring sun. Behind the manure piles swells a pond lushly fed by run-off from the barn yard. Even though it is not a true lake at all, this run-off pond is the only open body of water for thirty kilometres around. That makes it an important roadhouse for the birds, a staging point for their long flight north to their own gold rush. They drop in, exchange their horses, and are off again, or they spend the night, get a good meal, and shift off in the morning fog, their horses smelling of oats and sleep.

That's only in the spring, though. This unnamed meltwater pond evaporates all summer, until by mid-July the rippled, silver sheen of the water is just a small algal pool among reedy grasses and succulent waterweeds. By October it is a field of cracked mud and low, red weeds. They flame like paint squeezed out of a tube onto a palette—the scarlet an artist uses to paint a garter on a model's leg. The wind blows over the clay and you feel the cold of the coming winter and are exhilarated. In the spring, though, the pond is in its glory, thick with ducks, geese, swans, and horses. Yes. Horses. Cariboo horses.

The horses of the 105 are a peculiar breed. These are the cattle horses of the Monical Ranch. They are not pretty. Their coats are rough and tattered, their backs are swayed, their knees are knobbly, and they are used to a pretty tough life. They have to stand the incessant yapping of cattle dogs, to boot. These are horses with nerves of steel. They've stared down grizzly bears. They've tracked cows through clouds of mosquitoes. They've weathered lightning. They've seen it all. You cannot surprise horses like that. They'd be useless on the track, though. You couldn't spook them. They don't move fast, either. They wouldn't even bother competing against each other. Competition doesn't help you to survive in the bush. If you put the horses of the 105 in the cavalry, they'd stand around the edge of the battle, solemnly, wondering what all the fuss was. They think nothing of wading out in pond water, like moose, to munch on the water plants that sprout on the bottom in the early spring and float on the surface in the summer: duck food. They dip their heads right under and nibble off the tender shoots with their lips and bring them up, chewing on them contentedly. The wavelets on the water lap at their bellies. Cars whiz past, but the horses don't care. These horses are living in the Cretaceous. It wouldn't surprise me if they could speak Loon. ⇗

*I*n the last weeks of the woollen season, the hills are brown and grey like crumpled cigarette butts and the trees are grey and white like cigarette ashes and the firs are beginning to hint at the resurrection of the colour green (a kind of spit they suck out of chewing tobacco) and the ice of all the other lakes is bulging upwards as if it will explode at the centre of the lake into a geyser of water, a vast white flower opening in a city of jewellers and banks. It is then that the eagles come to the 105 pond. When they arrive, they are democrats. They are humanists. They have compassion for everyone in the world. No one believes a word of it, of course. This is Realpolitik, not a pipedream.

The thing is, birds have good memories. They remember the late spring and summer, when the eagles made a circuit over the lakes every day, looking for chicks or small adults to pluck up and carry dangling back to their young. They remember the fall, when hungrier eagles went after the ducks themselves. You don't trust people like that. They're like alcoholics stopping often to check the oil on their trucks because they've stashed a mickey of vodka behind the air filter. People like that are especially fond of goldeneyes. It might be because goldeneyes are white with black clown masks, a kind of circus costume that might make them dazzle under the big top but which out here on the plateau makes them so ridiculously easy to see. About all the coloration does for them is break up their outline. It's not a bad strategy when they're gathered together in a flock. An eagle diving on a flock of goldeneyes is going to get dizzy. He is going to get airsick. He will have to give up. The same doesn't hold for a single goldeneye, though. The eagles swoop on them over the reed beds, surprising them by droning in very quickly at a very low altitude, just skimming with their heavy bomb loads above the seed-heavy golden tops of the reeds. One minute the goldeneye is bobbing around on the edge of reeds, copper and red and purple with the cold of autumn, and the next it is dangling, and an eagle is flying heavily away, its wings bending and creaking with the strain, just on the edge of snapping in two.

Mind you, that behaviour only lasts a week. After that, the trails and the lake are littered with goldeneye feathers that catch and tremble in the slightest breeze, and the eagle spends his days in a dead poplar outside the old Clydesdale barn, staring wistfully at the water. A week is how long it takes for him to eat all of the stupid birds; he's completely unable to get any of the others. Survival of the fittest makes for an awfully tough life. You gorge yourself for a while, but then your stomach is pinched and rumbles and you'd do anything for a crust of mouldy bread.

No, in the summer and fall the other birds avoid the eagle like the plague, but in the spring they just ignore him. There's only one pond, and like a watering hole out on the Serengeti in the dry season, it's the only place open after 5:00 PM. The lion might be there in the grass, the hyenas might circle in the night, the leopards might be sleeping up in the trees, but lions and hyenas and leopards are only half as dangerous as death by thirst. ✣

Driven by their equal love of water, the geese and ducks and swans float and feed amongst the wading horses of the 105, as the wind ruffles the copper horses' dark, dank manes, and cows lie pregnant on the manure piles that flood the birthing yards. Big flakes of a late snow float down, rocking back and forth as they fall, as if they were cut out of paper in some school gym in another dimension and are materializing out of the air. It looks like a stage trick. It looks like God is making Himself manifest. When you look up, though, you can see that the flakes are the drift of a single cloud passing about a half kilometre to the west. Now, when I say *a single cloud* I don't mean a bit of fluff a child might draw above a crooked house and a crooked dog in a picture he makes in kindergarten and takes home to his mom on Mother's Day. In this big country, high up and above the world, a single cloud can be thirty kilometres across. That's what I mean. A cloud like that carries the water of a small fjord on the coast and dumps it inland, like a tanker truck washing down a gravel road in the sweltering heat of July. That's in the summer. In the winter it just carries a mountain of snow. It falls down your neck.

While traffic roars past on the highway, the spring eagles and geese and ducks stand without a thought for each other, shoulder to shoulder on the frozen mud rimming the meltwater pond of the Monical Ranch.

The ducks and swans and geese aren't paying any attention to the eagles, because the eagles are gorged on the afterbirth from the cows. The eagles look wise and ancient and proud and majestic. They are. They are standing there half asleep. When the sun warms the mud, they sink into the ooze. You can sometimes see them carry the afterbirth, big bloody masses of placenta and umbilical cord, across the holding pens, over the silver roar of semi-trailers hauling groceries and car parts into the North. They settle on the ice of 105 Lake across the road, where they tear at the placentas at their leisure. They have no need to be interested in other birds' potential as little spring rolls and Pizza Pockets, and so can hang around with them. They're just one of the guys. It is only later in the year, when hunger takes over, flipping dip switches inside the eagle's heads, that the eagles forget their manners, forget their brotherhood in the family of birds, and start to prey upon their springtime friends. It's a terrible way to live—a kind of perennial schizophrenia. Not only is the eagle not a noble bird, and a coward and an opportunist, too, but he needs therapy. Eagles are messed up. We should have compassion. They need a halfway house. They need BC Med. They need lithium pills by the bucketful. It's a scandal. ✢

When you see eagles flying in the summer, their recycled-billboard wings stretch out to the height of a man lying down on a park bench. In my case, it's even more than that. Up there, cut free from the earth, they are majestic and aloof. Well, that's what we've all believed for a couple hundred years, ever since this place was called Oregon and people told yarns about it, back when Thoreau was sitting beside his pond and seeing the movement of God in the trees and the water, and Johnny Appleseed was spitting out his apple cores at the side of a wagon trail. It's a way of looking at nature to see yourself. It's a way of writing a book of philosophy just by getting up in the morning. It's what you need to colonize a continent. That kind of thing can be addictive, though. It's like watching a Stephen Spielberg movie with its repressed anxieties, the ghosts that crop up in a mountain lodge because the place was built on an old, Indian graveyard. That's what wilderness has become: the bogeyman. He will come into your dreams with special effects and a lighting man.

You can't kill images like that. The idea of the noble eagle is one of them, part of the deck of cards that was played out in every bar from St. Louis to San Francisco, and from Oroville to Dawson City: romantic images of the Old West. (Sigh.) The deck was a series of paintings of craggy peaks and waterfalls where the untouchable spirit of the world, and hence the imagination, dwells. We're still dealing from that deck. Shelley could be writing his poems at your kitchen table right now. You could look up from whatever you're doing, peeling the spuds while Oprah natters at you, or watching a football game, and look with Shelley out the window, and nod, and he could dedicate the poem to you: "Ode to Freedom." God would shine a shaft of light down through the clouds, and an eagle would be flying there, high, in the face of storm. You would sigh in rapture in the face of the Sublime. You would understand the subtleties of starting words like *sublime* with a capital S. You would shake your head at people who don't understand those subtleties and who don't even know what the Sublime was, or is. You would talk about Freedom.

Whatever that freedom is, though—and, frankly, I don't have a clue—it has nothing to do with the eagle. The truth is, no matter how much we try to bend the facts to the idea of a God who can lift us to heights of clarity we can't even approach, eagles are simply not majestic. Aloof, rapacious, and moving with an incredible discipline of effort, certainly—sometimes moving at awe-inspiring speed with the power of the wind a kilometre above the lake, often exuding purpose—but never majestic. It is our ideas that are majestic. The eagles are just almond chicken on wings. Each one comes with a fortune cookie. They tell you your fate: if you're going to get married, if it's a good week to change jobs, that an unexpected opportunity is going to come your way. If you're in Ottawa, your fate comes in two languages. Fate signed the Charlettown Accord in Mandarin. There are eagles at Meech Lake. ⤳

In the summer, the neighbourhood eagle comes by at dawn, when the light is a dusty, pastel blue and deep purple shadows fall from the pines. Only the movement of the siskins among the clumps of cones on the branch tips brings the pines out of the dark shadows of their bulk—columns of night, standing long into the rising day. The lake glows with light, the reeds flush into colour, the sky beams orange and fuchsia, the grass rises from the earth again, the world wakes and stretches and goes about its business for hours, and only then does the light finally burn off the night in the pines. It evaporates from the needles like fog above the water.

In the half-light of dawn, the eagle appears among the pillars of the pines, banking among those towers of pure emptiness as if they are the canyons of Manhattan. Still in darkness, the waterbirds are crying on the lake. The eagle passes quickly, silently. He swings around again at 11:00 AM, when the light has risen to a deep yellow. The whole world has been dusted with goldenrod. Light lies over the face of the water and on the edges of grassblades, as if you could wipe it off with your finger. Light glows from within the honey tubes of the pine needles. It has been flavoured with cinnamon. The air is thick. ⤳

The ancient Greeks had a word for that thickening. They described it as an extension of the sun through the air. They called it *pneuma*—the soul. We are all part of that pneuma. We breathe it in. We breathe it out. As the Greeks saw it, pneuma is a liquid, present everywhere in the air, just as water is present everywhere within the ocean. Just like that water, at no point in the air was there any more light than there was at any other point. Their proof for its existence was that if you held your hand up in the light, the light flowed around it, like a mountain river around a boulder. Your hand didn't cut off the light because it didn't interrupt it.

The best time to swim in pneuma is midafternoon, between 3:00 and 4:00 PM—that time of day when the light is so thick in the air you push it heavily aside like a curtain as you walk. You feel it coursing down your throat as you breathe. It is hot and heavy and you move through it with great effort, as if you almost cannot bear its touch.

The eagle can. If you wipe the beads of light off your face with a towel and look high above in that clear expanse of colour that is both there and not there, you will see him, a dark shape planing in the agate-blue sky. He goes spiralling upwards on a thermal, framed against the distant bulk of thunderheads rising in the distance from the day's heating, forming a ring of mountains on the horizon like the Himalayas thrusting above the baked Indian plains. ✢

The eagle comes one last time at dusk, when golden light sweeps in low from the west like a last staging of Wagner's *The Ring*. All ruddy and golden, the reeds and aspens glow, lit by internal fires. At that hour, the light, pushed towards the red end of the spectrum by the relentless turning of the earth, glows within the leaves more intensely than it does in the air, unifying the whole world, like one of those squares of unpainted paper inside a water drop in a Walt Disney cartoon, with a star of light raying out from it: *ping!*

At dusk, with the light no longer glowing in the air, everything lit up with light glows intensely in and of itself. Each thing in the world, each tree or wheelbarrow or concrete brick, looks as if it is alone in the emptiness, as if it was created just as you saw it. It's then that the eagle comes for his last round, dressed up as one of Wagner's valkyries, with the music playing from speakers mounted on the side of his chopper, and his door gunner covering the tree line as he circles over the reeds. The world is a reel-to-reel tape deck. Believe it. ✦

The only time the eagle does not come is in the early afternoon, when the air is so saturated with light even a short journey around the lake or even just up the hill behind the house becomes a journey into the hills of the Hindu Kush, on foot, loaded down with ammunition and captured Kalashnikovs, taxing the body to its limit. The lungs don't even seem to grasp at the air. There's no oxygen in it. It is not a time for hunting but a time for sleep, and dreams. The eagle sits in his nest and stares at his collection of sticks. ✦

The eagle never gets to fly around without setting off every loon radar between here and Soda Lake, but he is persistent. You've got to give him that. He's like a computer hacker trying to break into the Pentagon's mainframe, running his password-crunching programs over and over again late at night, surrounded by coffee cups and computer cables. Eventually he gets lucky. Time and again, the loons confound the eagle's plan, yet he takes it in stride. Like a marijuana grow-op out under one of the haystacks in the bush by Forest Grove, powered by buried (and stolen) propane trucks, he knows it's just one of the costs of doing business. A fifty thousand dollar fine? A year in jail? Those are peanuts. The law is a circus. It relies on shame. Shame doesn't go as far as it used to.

It never went very far with the eagle. He comes back like clockwork. His trapline covers a hundred square kilometres of meadows, wetlands, lakes, and the forests and pastures between them. He even has a flyover above a Hydro transmission line and the long, straight clearcut of a natural gas pipeline. His life is one continuous ride above the air raid sirens. It probably has never struck him that a rising and falling wail riding across the whole audible range is not the regular, everyday, constant sound of the world. He checks his lakes and pastures four times every day, braving the DEW line of the loons, and the scramble of crows and blackbirds rising up like spitfires.

Bravest of all are the black terns. Their hunting territory is the foot of air above the surface of the lake, where they dip and swoop for mosquitoes within a hair's breadth of tumbling head over heels into the waves. When an eagle comes, they scramble up, out of the reeds and rise to his height, tiny specks like ashes blown on the fire-bombing of Dresden, dipping and turning, wheeling, caught in a wind. They're up there like Canada geese tossed in the exhaust of a stretched Hong Kong Airlines 747 landing in the fog at Vancouver International Airport. They're up there zipping around the eagle like electrons spinning around the nucleus of a crazy atom in Heisenberg's lab in 1942, when he was trying to make a bomb for Hitler, or trying to make it look like he was making a bomb so no one else would get the research funding and would actually make a bomb. These little electron terns, these plutonium terns, these enriched-uranium terns, these Messerschmitt terns, nip at the eagle. They force him to dip and roll, slicing the air with his big wings, almost out of control. His sense of grace is completely destroyed. It's all he can do to keep up in the air. He must feel like the crew of the spy plane that crashed into a Chinese fighter in the spring of 2001 and had to tumble down to a Chinese airfield like a potato chip bag dropped over the side of a ferry into oily water. The crew destroyed sensitive equipment with a fire axe all the way down: every computer user's dream! ⇒

The eagle is no fool. There is a point to his flybys, just as there is a point to the editorials in the *New York Times*, in the push-me-pull-you world of power and the sugar that's mixed with it on a spoon. The eagle's point isn't exactly pretty, either, but it is just as clever. The point was made to me in a storm, when it seemed like the trees in front of the house were going to shred away. Sheets of cardboard and stray plastic bags, branches, tumbleweeds, clouds of pollen, needles, dust, weeds, twigs, and birds went spewing past the window as if Sigourney Weaver had kicked out the airlock and the earth was being sucked into a big hole.

It started with the crows. Every day that entire spring, I watched a crow sail out from the aspens and over the reedbeds. The reeds were dark green, rising through burnished copper. The aspens were yellow-green, their new leaves sticky, half-sized, and still showing the crease-marks from where they had been folded again and again inside their beetle shells all winter. They trembled in a thousand facets in the slightest movement of air, like dresses of intricate cloth. The coolness of the water the aspens were drinking with their shallow, spreading roots from under the wildflowers was generating its own wind. They were motionless birds covered in green feathers.

Out in the reeds, the golden heads of the yellow-headed blackbirds sparkled like planets in a night sky, bright points of colour in a red-purple darkness. The female loon was hunched down on her muskrat nest, complete with her dock and waves broken up into low swells by their passage through the reeds. The male floated on the open water like Gilgamesh.

The crow made the flight every day. It was a milk run. You could set your watch by him. No sooner had he left the aspens on his slow, nonchalant flight, than a blackbird, red wingflakes flashing brightly, tore up from a willow, nipped at him, and drove him away. The crow lazily dipped and rolled to escape the blackbird, missing a wingbeat with each roll but otherwise flying right through the attack. After he had flown a hundred feet, the blackbird swung away, only to be replaced by another rising from the next willow, and the attack recommenced. Again the crow dipped and rolled, and again, after a hundred feet, the blackbird peeled away, only to be replaced by another, and so it went all along the sweep of the bay until the crow was lost to sight.

I had the distinct impression that the crow was doing all this out of sheer good humour, maybe even out of spite, trying to see what kind of rise he could get out of the little guys. You see that kind of thing all the time in junior high school hallways at lunch hour. Kids shove other kids into lockers, and laugh. Lunches are spilled. Everyone knows that if you go into the 600 hallway you will get beat up. It's as simple as that. Some things in life are not in shades of grey. It went on like this for weeks, and just when I was convinced that the crow had a truly memorable sense of humour—or a totally twisted one—I was shown the point of the whole exercise. ✢

The storm that morning rose suddenly out of the east. I had been following it on the radio. It had started in the south, where there was a storm warning in the Strait. From there, it moved up the trough of the Fraser Canyon, scattering trash in the roadside ditches of Boston Bar and Lytton, banging signs against poles and rattling windows. Farther north, among the abandoned apple orchards and derelict gas stations of

Spences Bridge, the storm had picked up the fine sand of the Thompson River and pelted it against windows like a hush of rain. In the wider valley around Ashcroft, with its abandoned tomato fields and feedlots and rail yards, it rattled over the microwave towers on top of the old sacred mountains. After that, the storm curved north and then almost immediately again west, as it peeled off against the southern slope of a high-pressure ridge coming down from Prince George.

Wind is an uncommon event here on the Plateau. Things are flat here. Tall mountains far to the east and west block out most extremes of weather. It simply passes overhead. You see its soft underbelly, like a snake, or a hundred snakes, gliding over you. The rising and falling of columns of air, so common in the mountain valleys to the east and south, does not occur here; the only regular wind we get is localized wind off of thunderstorms. Then there are the ocean storms. They sweep in from the Pacific, so huge that even after passing over the twenty-four-hundred-metre wall of the Coast Mountains and half-drowning the hemlocks on the western slopes of the peaks, they still surge three hundred kilometres inland to send garbage cans clattering and three-metre-tall canary grass spattering like bamboo against the window. A wind like that spills through the aspen leaves, setting them rustling and clattering, until the bright green trees are a blur, roaring like a brook running over mountain stones.

On the morning of the crow's big lesson, the wind was even stronger than that. It was the kind of wind that comes once in twenty years. It rose suddenly, tearing across the blue face of the lake in a grey shiver, followed instantly by a line of whitecaps. The pines shuddered down into their roots. The wind hit the reeds and sent them thrashing, crossing each other like swords in a Noh play full of ghosts and sadness, and hurled through the trees. More branches snapped off the big fir at the bottom of our path, and the loons were suddenly there in the green of shallow water a hundred metres off the brown curl of the reedbed, riding the white caps, facing into the cold wind, and calling, calling. This was not their distress cry. This was a cry of jubilation. The loons rose and fell on the waves as the smell of the lake—the pungent, burning sulphur smell of algae, the acid smell of mud and marsh, and the clear smell of rain—blew up through the writhing, thrashing forest. The world was a froth of movement; the only stillness in it was the loons, facing straight into the wind's mouth.

Then the lightning came. Thick rods of fire as thick as the trunk of a pine arced between cloud and earth. I didn't even have a chance to estimate the distance of the storm by counting seconds between lightning and thunder: they cracked and boomed simultaneously, as if the roof had blown off the house. I jumped out of my peaceful skin. The cat pushed itself into the darkest corner underneath the bed. The children screamed. As soon as the lightning struck, the sky burst into rain, and what a rain! Within a minute a sheet of water an inch deep was running down the road. My gutters drained in a continuous veil. More lightning, in big jagged forks branching out for kilometres over the lake, smashed down through the rain, again and again, draining its energy into the black water. Then, right in front of my window, amidst the strips of cardboard and the garden debris hurling over the roof, suddenly the crow was there, beating his wings furiously. He hurtled forward, desperately trying to keep control as the wind blasted him onward at such incredible speed. It was like having a rocket pack strapped to your back and trying to negotiate through the streets of Toronto. In other places you have to go to a special effects studio to get something like this. Here it's free.

The crow came past like a loose shingle, dipping and slicing through the air, yet he was not in distress: in his beak he held an egg. As fast as he had come he was out of sight again. I had little time to contemplate this apparition before the eagle came, too, again at great speed. Like the crow, he was tossed and buffeted by the wind. His wings were tense with the strain as he was jerked and torn through the air. In his claws was the rest of the nest, whatever nest it was, and he was driving his huge wings down against the wind, trying to keep aloft on the storm. A ride at Universal Studios couldn't outdo this. Disneyland has to eat its heart out over that afternoon on the Plateau.

By this time rain was driving on the wind in vast grey curtains of chain mail, and the entire lake surface was the colour of pitted grey steel. The reeds were lost, only a blur now, as the flash of their crossed motion meshed with the white haze of rain striking in at a low angle. As suddenly as the eagle had flashed into the blur of cloud streaming down the window, he was gone. Standing in the house that day was like driving a car at a hundred and twenty kilometres an hour down a mountain road in a thunderstorm. It was like watching *A Perfect Storm* by standing on the stage, a foot from the screen, as the action splashed out around you. You could have siphoned the adrenaline out of my blood and sold it on the street.

*A*s quickly as the storm came, it passed. A couple minutes after the crow and the eagle somersaulted in front of my living room window, the wind gave way from its fierce assault and dropped down to a steady push through the trees. The loons were still riding waves that passed under them and immediately stilled to smooth water in the blur of the reeds. The rain drove down, bouncing a foot off the soil, flattening the spring wildflowers into the grass.

A half hour later, the colours of the world were completely washed clean. Slower now, the wind no longer tore the crests off the waves. The whitecaps had vanished. The leaves of the aspens sparkled and tossed in yellow sunlight, and I stood there in a white wall of rain, jubilant, as rolling swells hissed among the reed stalks. I realized then that all this activity, all this daily passage over the willows, this offering of oneself to be attacked day after day, certainly had a lot to do with humour—it was a wild, long-running joke—but really had more to do with searching for food. It was a matter of knowing the location of every nest along the lake, so that when the right opportunity presented itself, the crow could be there, on the spot, ready to take full advantage of the situation when the defences of the lake were brought down or when a nest was torn out of a tree by the wind—whatever. ⤳

Sepa Lake is also the preferred love nest of coots. Now, there's a crazy bird. Coots look like miniature sealskin boats. That's on a good day. On a bad day they look like little gumboots bobbing on the water. On a really bad day they look like blobs of tar from an oil spill. They're completely waterproof, at any rate. The little guys are about fifteen inches long, with bright white bills like plastic clothespins. Their young look like fluffy, grey slippers, the kind you find showing up next to the till at discount stores at Christmas, in animal shapes—elephants and rabbits and mice. They're hung up on racks next to the till because they're not something you would buy when you were in your right mind or had a few minutes to think about it. Those are not slippers you wear. Those are slippers you laugh over. Those are Christmas slippers. Those things are art. Coots, who like living on the edge, are performance artists. Coots might look comical, but they're tough. The phrase "crazy as a coot" didn't spring up out of nowhere, and it's not because they've run out of their prescriptions and the pharmacy is closed until March. It's just that they like the cold. They really like the cold.

Coots are waterbirds. They make the loons look like town folk who only come down to the Government Wharf on Thursdays to buy some prawns or Coho salmon off the boats, with the rust bleeding down the sides of the hulls like teriyaki marinade. Coots don't have any use for land whatsoever. They live among reeds. They build their nests on floating reed platforms, like you might see shifting sanguinely down the Congo River, messing up the propellers of steamers and making their way into travel adventure books by eccentric Englishmen chasing birds: wall-to-wall deep pile carpets of reeds driven together by waves and wind and held together by the warp of the reeds growing up through them. Kings of these rattan-flooring empires, coots pretty much keep to themselves.

Eagles, on the other hand, look at coots the way we eye Black Forest hams lined up in the coolers at Safeway in Williams Lake, all plump in their little vacuum-pack bags: discounted five bucks to Safeway Club members. It's true: eagles look at those reed platforms as freezers that you store downstairs in the furnace room, with the air blowing around them and spider webs waving. Eagles are very suburban. They are living the good life. *

Long after the eagles are gone for their winter spa vacations and time-shares in Howe Sound, however, the coots are still hanging around, their Russian leather and sheepskin caps pulled down around their ears and buttoned up tightly under their chins. Freeze-up is their time to shine. It's summer that they have a hard time with, all bundled up tight in their wetsuits, without a chance for their bodies to breathe and stretch.

By freeze-up, though, all the other birds have left. It is a slow exodus, but a relentless one. Species by species, day by day, birds disappear from the Plateau. It starts with the swallows in mid-July, and ends with the big birds—the loons in September, the mergansers and ducks in October.

In the end, only the coots are left, bobbing around on the lake like the caretakers at a summer resort in the Shuswap after Thanksgiving, going about their business, boarding up the windows, taking in the canoes, tipping the picnic tables over, raking leaves and spending the evenings drinking rye whiskey and playing Rummoli as the cold fronts move down one after another from the North. All spring and summer the coots are scattered discretely around the lake and throughout the other sets of the eagle's trapline—the smaller lakes up in the bush, circular pools of water ringed by reeds and aspens. As the bush pools freeze, the coots come down out of the hills. As our lake closes in with ice until only the wind-driven bays along the north shore are open, all the coots in the neighbourhood swim together. When the fall nights are especially cold, dropping down to minus ten or minus twelve Celsius overnight and the lake gels around their feet, the coots keep their water open by swimming around in it day and night. They swim in circles, in a tightly choreographed movement.

One November, I watched the coots as the fog rose from the western slope of each wavelet, caught the wind, drifted for a few feet, and dissipated in the air. Against that perfectly balanced dance of water and atmosphere, the coots had gathered in groups of four for a big synchronized swimming competition. Within their groups, they turned in circles, in position, with the pair from each opposing corner turning counter-clockwise to each other. There were over thirty birds on the lake, all synchronized, not only within their small groups but between groups as well. It was like watching square dancing on the big, plywood stage they used to put up in Penticton every summer. As a whole, the movement of the groups was arranged in the same pattern as the birds within the individual dancing groups of four. I was looking at pure mathematics.

Occasionally an entire group of four dancers dove under the water and reappeared elsewhere in the bay, where they bobbed up and down on the waves for the moment before resuming their dance. Even this diving was synchronized. The choreographer had worked for a long time on this number. You could tell by the attention to detail.

Although over time each group dove, for the entire duration of the dance the pattern on the lake maintained its symmetry. I swear it was the dance of creation itself, something that usually plays out at too slow or too fast a speed for us to follow: the lifting and settling of hills as continental plates shift against each other under our feet like old lovers in a Downtown Eastside rooming house, or the quick seething masses of starlings rising out of hayfields, condensing on power lines, and swirling and scattering into the sky like disappearing time—the whole film of life sped up way too much. With the coots, though, the speed is right for us. They move in slow motion on a lake just on the verge of freezing and that would have frozen days before if it were not for their activity. They love this place intensely, with its wide, white skies and torn ocean clouds that have come three hundred kilometres inland, yet still smell of rain on a packed clay shore rimmed with salt hay. They love it so intensely that they cannot bear to leave.

They eventually do, of course, sadly, tearing themselves away as the last ice crystals close up around their feet. They don't go to California or Mexico, though. They stay as close as they can, fleeing south to the Okanagan, where the deep valley shrouded in fog is protected from the worst of the winter cold. I have seen the coots there in the concrete-grey winter winds of Penticton, with its wind-scoured motels, their vacancy signs banging, and knapweed and tumble mustard skittering down the wide, empty tourist streets, with grey, wind-blown snow clotting up in the pools of the water slide. The coots were bobbing around in big flocks of hundreds of birds, swimming in absolutely no set pattern at all in the dredged Okanagan River channel between the Indian reserve and the highway. In the summer, the channel is thick with families from Vancouver and Calgary and Red Deer, floating on inner tubes down next to the Highway 97 Bypass, turning pink and lobster-red among the loosestrife.

In the winter, the coots come, in the roar of traffic and the boom of planes rising and falling at the airport. With their funny hats and goggles in the incessant howl of wind loaded with Skaha Lake sand, the tourist coots swim there in the sewage effluent, looking so warm they're almost sweating in their head-to-toe wet suits. In the long months of snow, when for those of us on the Plateau the rest of the world ceases to exist in the imagination, it is good to see them there, old friends lost and met again. Summer might be nothing more than a margarita recipe in the patio drinks book, a half-empty bottle of sunscreen above the bathroom sink, and a few photographs of kids bobbing in the turquoise water—that film that you found in the camera at Christmas with one shot still to snap. You look at it as if it happened on another continent. You look at it as if it happened to someone else. Outside, the snow falls. It falls and falls, and slowly you lose the belief that the world will come again. It always has so far. Mind you, as the coots would point out: it always leaves. ⇥

One summer, my daughters and I drove through a twenty-kilometre-long hailstorm between 100 Mile House and our home on the 108 Mile Ranch. The mixed hail and rain came down so thickly that at 105 Mile it was impossible to see a thing. I stopped my car in the middle of the road and waited it out—I couldn't even see to pull over to the shoulder, and could only see the car ahead once we were twenty feet away. Even then it was nothing more than a dim red glow from its taillights. Water lay an inch deep over the road. Where driveways intersected the highway on a hill, the water increased to three inches. All the hayfields were white. The cattle stood around, shocked. Similarly, a week and a half before Easter in 1998, I was driving my daughters past the 128 Mile Marshes, where the highway cuts across the bends of the Cariboo Wagon Road. Watching the old track wind around the hills, I thought of the miners who had walked there through the snow. Those guys knew loneliness. Then I saw the herons. Two blue herons were standing like old, twisted stumps of trees flooded by a beaver dam, dried out by twenty years of sun. Blue-grey moss and lichen hung off them in tatters.

To see a blue heron fly is like seeing an umbrella take wing—a rickety, impossible business. Blue herons have long wings inherited from their second cousins on their mother's side, the pterosaurs, and legs stretching behind like a child's drawing tacked up in a school hallway. As far as birds are concerned, these guys are the Orville and Wilbur Wrights of the aviation business, but they do fly, and they can really move. Each beat of those flimsy wings, with the canvas stretched tightly over spruce crossbeams and tied together with wires and cables and struts, takes them twenty yards.

The ones out on the 128 Mile swamp, though, were going nowhere. They stood in interstellar stillness on the mottled white ice of late spring. Along the highway, the starlings clustered on the power wires, but below them the herons stared into a single hole in the ice, two yards across. White shoals of snow drifted against the hills kilometres to the south, and the cold from it wafted over the birds and buffeted my car. The birds stood there as if they have always stood there, holding a secret so old we have lost it, a stillness matched only by the stillness of the ice around them, as the world drifted in movement and I hurtled down the road into a wall of snow. Small round balls of snow the size of those silver-coated sugar balls you can buy in little plastic tubes in the baking section at Safeway and use to decorate a wedding cake bounced around me as they drifted across the road. ⟶

Spring snow catches at the heart. It is completely different than autumn snow—or winter snow. It is impermanent. It lies over the world like the flowers from a plum tree shading a carp pond in a temple garden in Japan: tended for a year; blooming for a day.

Usually, spring snow is just the will of a single cloud. It settles down over you almost like a personal blessing from the old God of romantic landscape painting. You feel like you are in a Victorian Valentine's Day card, with roses around the edge, and little cherubs blowing you kisses, with ribbons and gilt accents and a blush of pink.

Just as I entered the snow at 128 Mile and the angels started clearing their throats, getting ready to sing "That Old Rugged Cross," just as my windshield wipers started to sweep the snow off in front of me and squeak against the glass—the snow was that dry—I saw two swans, white, their heads and bills black, necks outstretched, coming in low over the San Jose River, above the backs of Belgian workhorses up to their withers in umber grass. There was very little light left in the air and what there was had been swallowed by the storm. The air had become a form of electricity. It was a liquid, moving between the swans and herons and horses and me, joining us together. Immersed in it, the swans shone, as white as the moon, flying down to the water at long, slow angles. They were landing for the night, to rest for a day and then fly on, pond by pond, lake by lake, north, outracing the spring. ⟶

We are all travelling. One morning, the girls and I found the eagle nest. I had taken them for a walk up onto the ridge above Sucker Lake, where the cliff falls off like the escarpment of Africa's Great Rift Valley and the dwarf blue junipers spread under the trees among the first wildflowers. It was a long walk through mud, old snow, rock, old snow, and again mud. Halfway back, when the girls were making noises that we'd never find our way back and I was beginning to think that at our speed they were probably right, we found the nest. It was in an old fir snapped by lightning, up against the ridge south of Sucker Lake and at the head of the spawning channel—a big mess of branches two metres across and almost a metre thick. The branches of the fir curl up around the nest. It looks like they have been doing so for about forty years. The eagles have an easy view of the lake from there, and of the highway, too, grey and silver. Even the big trucks are silent at that distance. The wind swooshes through the branches. I imagined living up there, thinking of those subdivision signs that sprout up out of the bracken east of Vancouver: "If you lived here you'd be home." ✣ ✣ ✣

Colonel Watson's Swallows

The swallow sweeps
The slimy pool, to build his hanging house.
  ⇒James Thomson

I love to live near water. I love to have a view down over it, through trees—aspens, if possible, with their trunks full of mountain bluebird nests and their branches humming with paper wasps. I love to sit among these trees, and to still myself to their slow breathing and the rightness of the mathematical placement of wood and water across the soil. I don't think of the water as my home, though. It provides a net for life. I am caught by that net.

It's not the same for the herons and the ducks, the loons and geese, the coots, grebes, and cranes, the swans and buffleheads, the teal, widgeons, and sandpipers who come in and out of my days. For them it is a planet of water. To grouse, it is a planet of tree trunks receding as far as the eye can see, without the trees themselves or any perspective or distance—just tree trunks standing up like fences planted in a crazy field, tree trunk after tree trunk after tree trunk, jammed together like birthday candles in a helluva big cake: tree trunks and dead grasses, a world of twigs and old leaves and tangles of rosebushes and dried lily stems pushing up through snow turned to ice by the winter sun. On cloudy days, a grouse's world is a series of snowless clearings under big firs. Grouse see the world as pure geometry. The geometry is a place to hide in. Rabbis studying the Kabala are not so pure of heart, nor so focused. The harsh geometry of the desert is not so pure. Grouse are the birds of the earth.

In the hard winter of 1949, just before the flood that almost washed civilization out of every river valley in British Columbia, the snow fell so long and hard that all the grouse under Hudson's Bay Mountain west of Smithers sheltered under bushes to keep dry. Once the snow stopped falling, it rained. As it rained it froze, encasing the bushes in thick shells of ice. Unable to escape from those shells, the grouse all suffocated.

My mother was fourteen years old then, under that mountain, where she lived and suffocated in a log cabin and milked the cow while mice squealed in the hay overhead. Out of pity she went out into the deep snow with her dog and kicked open the bushes one by one, and one by one the dog rushed into them and dragged out the dead birds in his mouth, his tail wagging excitedly, but not one of the birds was still alive. →

I have a theory about grouse. Natural selection is tough for all living things—the point is that it's tough—but in the case of grouse, it's tougher. With grouse, it practically hits them over the head with a 2 x 4. Here's how it works. For protection, grouse have two things in their favour. The first is perfect camouflage. If a grouse decides not to move, it is pretty well impossible to tell it from an old fir stump. A grouse's feathers are layered exactly like the flakes of old dead bark on a stump and the dead leaves surrounding it. The other thing that grouse have going for them is the element of surprise, coupled with the ability to accelerate from zero to fifty kilometres per hour in about one second flat. The thing they have going against them is their intelligence: they don't have any.

Life, you see, for a grouse, is a lot like playing Russian roulette. When you come upon a grouse—standing in the weeds and the dried leaves that fell like molten gold the previous fall and turned grey over the winter, you don't see the grouse, unless it moves. It usually moves. I mean, a grouse will try to stand still, because that is its most excellent camouflage, but when you get too close, say within two metres, it bolts. At two metres, it will strut sideways through the bush, dipping under fir boughs or sliding into a thicket of rose bushes and soapberries, to disappear. It is as if it had walked through a veil between worlds, into the land of the queen of the faeries, where all that is invisible becomes visible and all that is visible becomes invisible. Our world is made out of so many worlds like this, all fit into and sliding through each other—so many universes of interlocking perception, web upon web cast across the planet, wrapping her up at night as the stars rain down over the shoulder of the land.

If you are closer than two yards, though, the grouse explodes underfoot and hurtles away through the trees like a surface-to-air missile: fired blindly in panic, at the last possible moment. Therein lies the salvation for the grouse and its damnation, because it's tough to explode forward like that and preserve yourself, no matter how quick your reflexes. There's the grouse, hurtling forward like the space shuttle re-entering the atmosphere: at speeds like that, it has no control. It's the first second of re-entry into the grouse's world that is the most difficult, because in that first second the grouse's wings are accelerating the grouse, but not steering it. In other words, the grouse is flying blind, accelerating on a high curve, faster and faster and faster with every millisecond. Only after that first critical second does the grouse have a chance to fire its retrorockets, adjust its wing feathers, and guide itself, by the touch of a feather on one side or the drop of one on the other, as it careens wildly through the trees like a souped-up Chevy at the Nlaka'pamux Eagle Motorplex in Ashcroft, with the young bucks taking in the cash at the gate and dropping the chequered flag.

God help any grouse which hits a tree in that first second, because it won't even see what's coming, as it is hurled deep within itself by the G forces as it breaks through the atmosphere and smashes into the tree, and that is that. All goes black. A stillness hangs over the forest. ⤳

I found a grouse like that once, twitching beside my house. I had been working on an early draft of this book in the cool of the basement when there was a mighty thump on the wall. I went outside to see what on earth was going on. Well, I saw all right. A grouse was dying there on the lawn between the three-metre-tall canary grass and the vinyl wall of the house, that's what. The grouse was in the last throes of death, and the orange cat was walking towards it out of the canary grass. I told the cat what I thought.

"What on earth are you doing?" I said to him, as he curled his tail and twitched it at the tip and stepped forward inquisitively, the fat on his shoulder rippling. This was a cat who did not need to go hunting birds like this, but hunt him he did, out of sheer curiosity, and the bird had panicked and hit the house before it could count to one. "You might at least finish him off," I said.

The cat looked at me. "No way," he said. "Wow. Do you see how big that thing is? Wow."

"Well," I said, standing over the now-dead bird as it lay on the grass and the bee-yellow sun swarmed over us all and the swallows chirred from their mud nests up under the roof and the heat was warm on my back. It was the first real day of spring. "Well, if you're going to kill a bird like this, you should at least eat him."

"Who? Me?" said the cat. "No way. That thing's big."

So I picked the cat up and lifted him over to the bird, and held his nose to the bird's still-warm head, and he pushed the bird away and scampered off a few feet.

"No way. I'm not eating that. Do you see how big it is?"

"Fine," I said. "I'm not going to waste a bird like that," and I took it into the kitchen to deal with it myself. ✦

$\mathcal{M}$y friend Wayne—the Buddhist beekeeper and organic orchardist and vegetarian breadmaker from Cawston, where the soapstone spills out of the cliff and the red-tailed hawks nest as the lichen blooms green on the shale—once told me about skinning grouse. I was hunting roosters in his orchard with a flashlight. The roosters were actually fighting cocks, because Ivan's fighting cocks had come across the road and mated with Wayne's chickens. Ivan kept fighting cocks so that they would stand a chance against the rattlesnakes and coyotes and hawks that came down for them from the mountain, where the ant lions laid their traps and the bears plunged down at night to eat the chancellor grapes out of their neighbour's vineyard.

"How can you stop a rooster from doing what a rooster has to do?" asked Wayne.

You can't.

Wayne kept chickens so they would scratch under his trees and eat the codling moth larvae that dropped down there to incubate. Wayne's whole orchard was a wild chicken run, with little chicken houses the size of spaniel houses under the trees, and holes where the chickens had made dust baths. Ivan's randy cocks bred with Wayne's bantam hens. The result was an overpopulation of roosters.

"They can be skinned exactly like a grouse," said Wayne, no more than a whisper and a smell of garlic in the darkness next to me. "You just have to loosen the skin around the neck, and the whole pelt slips off like a glove. You can sell the feathers to someone who wants to use them for fly-tying."

I heard that, there in the night, as I slipped on rooster shit and climbed up ladders, a heavy leather glove on my right hand, seizing roosters by the feet and hauling them down screaming and kicking out of the trees. I felt like some Hopi kid five hundred years ago, climbing up a butte to catch young eagles to raise them so he could use their feathers for sacred ceremonies, to build spells to spill his soul out wide into the drama of the air.

I tried that with my cat's grouse. It didn't work. I mean, it probably was a good idea, and if I'd had someone to show me what to do I could have pulled it off. As it was, I pulled it off, all right. I pulled the skin off in big clumps and stuffed them into the garbage under the sink, and there I had it: two tiny legs, negligible wings, and a huge breast. The meat was in the breast, but it was only enough for one person, and we were four. I wrapped it up and put it into the fridge, cleaned up the feathers, which had floated all over the kitchen, wiped down the blood, took the stinking guts out to the garbage, and then stepped back out to the canary grass. The cat was still there, sunning, right next to the water puddle where the swallows were dipping down for more mud. Next to him, bees were humming in the pussy willow, swarming around the bush like the Andromeda Galaxy. The bush was rich with yellow pollen, in long, heavy catkins, like earrings or jewels, and the bees moved over them from bloom to bloom to bloom. That's where I bent down and had a talk with the cat.

"Chuck," I said. "That was good. You're a good cat. You're a good hunter. Now I want you to go out and get three more of those things.

I need enough for everyone in the house."

He yawned and stretched. That night I served one grouse breast, and three chicken breasts to finish out the meal. ⇥

For the black terns, the earth is a planet of air. Angels bringing messages from an unseeable, unknowable God are more their cup of tea, not the geometry of the body, moulded out of clay, dried in the desert sun and struck with the hand like a bell.

W. B. Yeats, the Irish poet, and his secretary Ezra Pound, the cranky American poet, used to spend the winters of World War I in the fog of Surrey, England, inventing modern verse while the fire crackled in the grate and the damp dripped from the rafters. After World War I, they tried to warm up by sitting in the hills of St. Ambrogio, Italy, looking down over the Rapallo harbour below the steep, terraced hills. All the time, they watched swallows swooping through the light in front of them. In those days no one believed in anything anymore, except revolution and its suppression, but since this new world was all so fresh to them, they still went through the forms of the old. Men wore suits and spats. Princes wore men. It was a terrific time to be a poet. Poets still dreamed of the land. God had already been declared dead, Christ had already been buried in Ypres and Verdun, but a poet could still believe in angels, in the magical power of jewels, and in the shallow space separating us all from the world of the divine. The world could still be a riddle and a mystery and a work of art, and industry was still, at times, a poem. It was fading fast, under the onslaught of mechanized death and the cynicism of power, but it had not gone yet. The physicists had not yet split the atom. They had not yet changed the way we speak to God: one to one. We still spoke to other men back then, and left any afternoon chat with God, over tea and crumpets, to the poets. The poets rose to the challenge.

And so while the people, shell-shocked, walked away from the poets into their factories and tenements, stoop-shouldered, grey-faced, the poets watched the swallows. To everyone else, the world was hell, with all the young men dead and everyone else sick with influenza or holed up in a sanatorium in the alps, even a few crazy Finns fishing at the mouth of the Fraser River in British Columbia, but to the poets the world was a direct video link to God.

It has all become commonplace now. God has His own SMTP server now. We transcend the earth with technology today, with USB sticks, dial-up modems, and fibre optic cables, with firewires and firewalls and satellite dishes and handheld GPS devices. Back then, the poets did it with their minds. What God thought, whatever God might be, however deeply He might be buried in the universe, whatever primal force He might be, whether He was what the physicists would later describe as the Big Bang or not, was instantly mirrored in the swallows swaying through the evening air of St. Ambrogio. There was absolutely no processor delay. The flick of a wingtip was a surge of thought. The lift of a voice in song, or in a poem, was the same impulse. The divine flooded the air. The poets swam in it. They drank it. It washed over them. They could hardly see through it to any other world. When people moved in front of them, they moved like bolts of cloth seen through clouds of dust in a weaving shop lit by high overhead windows in 1500s Flanders.

Well, times have changed. The physicists took over the game. It's not so easy to be a poet anymore, but in their takeover, the physicists missed the birds. Here on the Plateau, the black terns fill the space of Yeats' Italian swallows, which looked like they were flying right out of a fresco, that even spoke Italian in coos and trills, those opera swallows, those tenors and sopranos, those ice cream salesmen and organ grinders and cappuccino drinkers of swallows, those Neapolitan swallows and Sicilian swallows and swallows dreaming of Vespas and gnocchi, all flying out of the walls of a church and back into it again, materializing out of stone and becoming the movement of a hand over wet plaster and frozen in time. ⇗

The terns are not flying out of a fresco. They are Canadian birds. They are small, thin birds with black breasts and heads and razor-sharp wings spreading about twelve inches. When they first arrive in the spring, they are about eighty percent white. They look like chips of foam splashing up into the air, dancing above the wave-tips. After a few days of feeding above the lake, that colour darkens to soot, and as soot the terns live out the summer: the shadow between wave and wave. They come every spring as the mayflies start to hatch. Dipping and swirling in wide swarms, filling the whole space from one foot to two hundred feet above the lake in a dancing, ever-shifting movement, they feed from the first moments of dawn to the last failing shadows of dusk, when they can just be made out against the pale violet glow of the central dome of the sky. This is not the dome of St. Peter's, though: that is an imitation of this older, purer expanse. The terns dart to this side and that and up and down, catching insects like angel wings shining darkly on the light that surrounds them. The light is their ocean, the first ocean of the world, the one God's Word raced across, the sun breaking above the water and shooting across the wavetops, and the world rising triumphantly out of night. ⇗

The terns have a thin cry that carries across the sky as if it is pushed through a long, thin reed in a cold wind. These are birds that never touch down on the soil—or the water. When they rest at night, they rest on the reeds. Their nests are fastened to the reeds with their spit. These guys and gals hold the original patent for Krazy Glue. The earth is a foreign country to them. If the essence of being a bird is to fly, then the black terns of the Plateau are very pure—as easily read as the Torah and all the rabbinical commentaries on it down through the centuries. You read them as words rendered purely, lifted up, riding the light as the rain pours down the windows. ⤷

You don't hear catchy jingles about angels on the radio these days. You don't see slogans about angels published in the business section of the *Globe and Mail* during a federal election. You don't hear the most recent stock price for angels after the CBC Morning News. At most, you'll find something about angels in the Lifestyles Section in the newspaper of a medium-sized city like Calgary or Victoria, a city more tied to toasters and all-season tires than to seraphim and the ordered layers of purity suspended from the perfection of God. There is a long distance between the manifestations of spirit as steel-belted rubber and the air within the air within the air.

It used to all be the same thing. During the Barkerville Gold Rush, a clerk at a chocolate shop in Victoria, BC, had to vouch for his morality if he was to have a job doing the books late at night. Having a girlfriend was completely out of the question. It is a wonder the human race managed to procreate. In those colonial times, there was a unity between the romantic world of mountains and the utilitarian world of business. They came together in the lives of prospectors, crawling over every likely rockface in the province. They founded mines, too, all over: at Hedley, at Princeton, at Kimberley, at Nelson. Towns and cities sprang up, with amateur dramatic societies and gingerbread houses and dirt streets. Travelling theatre groups came by on tour from the United States. People drank themselves silly. Then the mines dried up.

Before long, swallows nested in the mud walls of the old tailing ponds and rose up into the light, their bodies humming with arsenic. And then came the big adventure: the War in Europe. Millions of men were machine-gunned trying to cut their way through barbed wire in a sea of mud and choking gas, while skylarks flew up above them, twittering about eternity. ✦

I looked up into the light this morning and I noticed that the terns were flying around in the reeds like a swarm of mosquitoes, crying and shrieking. They were circling above a canoe that two boys were paddling through their nesting grounds, the shallow, snail-rich water among the reeds. The boys were ten years old, and were completely unfazed by the upset birds. They just sat there in their fiberglass canoe as a slow wave rocked the boat back and forth and the reeds banged the sides of the boat like hollow, wooden wind chimes. The reeds swung around the boys slowly, dipping and rising with the water. The closer the water was to shore, the more still it grew. The sun shone.

One boy hung onto the gunwales. The other was resting his hands on his paddle, which he had laid across the canoe like a silver knife across a dinner plate after a Christmas feast. The cries of the birds didn't carry over the willows and up to our house. It was all taking place in such silence it was unreal, like a movie recorded on an old Super 8 camera with the focus pulled way back, and no mic. The boys were hardly moving. I turned from them for a moment and called to Diane to come and see what was going on.

When I turned back to look at the boys again, they still hadn't moved. The part of the world where they had found themselves was frozen in relation to the world where the terns and I were living. The reeds swayed around the boys, but the boys did not move. The terns were swarming around them like a cloud of gnats above damp sand. Still the boys did not move. If the terns were having a conversation with God it was a hot one, but it was taking place where the boys could never hear it. Only a minute passed before Diane came out on the deck. The sun glared off the white railing, throwing light upward over our faces, making us squint. We could hardly see. It was so bright there were scarcely any shadows for the light to cast a shape against. It was hot, too. Pressed between the railing and a wall of windows, we were in an oven. God was throwing on coals.

"I'll get the binoculars," I said, and slipped inside through the kitchen. In contrast to the brightness outside, inside it was dark as night. As my eyes adjusted for a moment, I walked in a fog through the vague outlines of shapes in darkness. By the time I got back outside with the binoculars Diane was agitated. She snatched the binoculars from me as soon as I came close and looked out with them over the water. She spent a long time watching—too long, it seemed to me, for the boys were starting to move forward through the reeds and the birds had gone completely crazy. The boys' world had meshed with ours again. God had finished talking. What we were seeing now was what He had to say about it. ✣

I was a boy once myself. I know a boy's need for adventure and defiance. I know how he needs to become hard, and how he fails at it and learns compassion. The birds were racing around the boys like a swarm of hornets when you throw a rock at their hive. That was something else I knew. When I was ten years old myself, I hadn't messed with terns, but I had messed with hornets. I hadn't even known there was such a bird as a black tern. I had never even been to a mountain lake. My target, instead, was a big, black hornet nest hanging on a high limb of an apricot tree along the bank from our house. My friends and I rode our bicycles through the dust of the farm, our pockets filled with rocks, chips of shale that had been hauled in to fill in the driveway that sank down into the muck every spring and was renewed every summer. The driveway was a metre deep with rocks, but it was still rutted. Our pockets were heavy and scratchy against our thighs.

When we got close to the tree, we threw our bikes down, ran forward through the scrubby weeds, and started throwing. Our plan was simple: as soon as one of us hit the nest, we would get on our bikes and ride away. We'd be safe, because of our speed. We were proud of our speed. That was the whole point of the exercise with the hornets: that we knew how fast we were, so we were completely protected.

In the end, we weren't that speedy and we sure weren't safe. We had forgotten about pride, of course. That was our undoing. Everyone wanted to be the one who hit the nest, so once the nest started shredding under the rocks, once the hornets started pouring out of it in rage and swept through the trees, funnelling towards us like bullets out of a Gatling gun, we all kept throwing, to make sure that it was our rock that hit the nest, the magic rock that left our fingers and flew through the air on an invisible string to tie us directly to the nest. Without that, we would not share, not properly, in the excitement of the game. As a consequence, however, we stayed too long—far, far too long.

With a swarm of very angry hornets coming for me, what seemed like such a quick and simple thing—mounting a bicycle and riding away on it—became interminably slow. I was riding away in slow motion. As slow as a man made of lead walking into the reactor chamber at Chernobyl, I got my bike up off the ground, and slowly, ever so slowly swung my leg over the bar, and ever so slowly, and with the greatest exertion, lifted my foot to place it on the pedal. All the while the hornets were bearing down on me almost at the speed of light, so large, magnified by my fear, that they seemed like small sparrows. They got me before I even got my foot in place. They stung my head and shoulders, my arms and my neck and my hands. Shouting, slapping and yelling, and jerking where they stung me, I tucked my head down and rode off, at first slowly, then faster and faster. All the time, the hornets were at me, furious.

They weren't just after me, either. They chased us all like that for two hundred yards, then peeled away, flying in large defensive swoops through the whole lower section of the apricot orchard, black, darting suddenly out of the air, then disappearing into it again. It's not something you forget easily. These terns looked just as upset as those hornets had been, and the boys looked, well, like ten-year-old boys. I didn't think there was any great mystery here.

"Can I have the binoculars now?" I asked.

Diane handed them to me. As I looked, two canoes and two reedbeds floated up before me: one lifted up above the other, in the sky; the other, where it should have been, in the lake, superimposed upon a sky of trees and houses.

"They have something in their canoe," Diane said quickly. "What are they doing?"

Damned if I knew. As I've said, they weren't very good binoculars. They were garage sale binoculars. When I first got them, they did see in stereo. For a few years that continued. Then we moved to the lake, where they were in constant demand. At the lake, the kids had dropped them a few times. The mounting frame was cracked. The tubes were out of alignment. I watched intently, terns flitting through my field of vision, close, as their cries floated up faintly.

"They are throwing something," I said at last, letting out my breath. I could make out that much.

"No," Diane said, drawing the word out. She turned to me. "How can people do such a thing?"

I didn't tell her about the hornets. "I don't know," I said.

Diane took the binoculars from me and I watched the birds without them again. There were half as many. Now that I could see the whole flock, I saw that the boys were not hurting the terns. I could also see that the terns were very upset.

"It's something white," she said, passing the binoculars back.

As I looked again, Diane started shouting. "Hey! HEY! Get away from there!" She was leaning way over the railing and waving her hands, crossing them in front of herself like a big "Train Crossing" sign.

The boys lifted their heads, then started paddling again, slowly, leisurely.

"HEY!" Diane yelled, more loudly than I had ever heard her yell before.

"You know," I said, as the sun burned into my eyes. "I don't think they care."

Diane looked fit to kill.

"It looks like they've collected some eggs from the nests and are throwing them at the birds," I said.

Diane turned deathly white.

"They're probably afraid," I said. I meant the boys.

Without saying a word, Diane marched off the porch, and down the trail through the larkspurs and paintbrush. I watched her progress through the binoculars: first Diane, then the canoe, then, as the canoe became screened by the willows, Diane alone. There, in her blue coat, with the water lapping around her feet, Diane called to the boys again. They gave no response, but they did stop throwing, and paddled slowly away into the open water. The waves lifted and dropped the canoe between each stroke of the paddles.

The terns were upset for a whole half an hour after that, until the tightly knotted swarm gradually loosened up, just as those hornets had done so many years ago through the red branches of the apricot trees. The terns began to fly in wider and wider circles over the water until they were covering the whole surface of the lake with their arcs and their anger had given way to their watchful hunting. The lake was alive. Something of the lake had lifted up into the air with the terns, and was large and full of energy.

And the terns are so beautiful when they fly, cutting mathematically elegant curves and vectors through the air, falling from great height, then catching themselves on their wings in perfect arcs, even if extinction is so close and our lives are all so precarious.

Diane and I were shaken for the rest of the day, so keyed up with tension that our arms and chests ached. We got absolutely nothing done. We hurt. ✸

Like the terns, the swallows ride the air high above the house in broad swoops as if each one of them is swinging from a string anchored to a different point in the air. Like ghosts soaring through a production of *Fiddler on the Roof,* or the choreographed fighters of *Crouching Tiger, Hidden Dragon,* the swallows fall into the deepest part of their dives, flatten out, and rise at the same speed. They float effortlessly, as if they could ride there forever, as if they were soaring on strains of music. The lowest swallows swerve just over the roof, where the light catches the mosquitoes like small, incandescent wires. The highest ones are unexpected. You look up and see only air. You don't see swallows, then suddenly you do see them: past what you thought were the highest swallows in the air you see swallows still higher—dark, drowned out in the brightness of the upper sky. At that distance they are smaller than the incandescent mosquitoes above the house. It is as if with nothing to focus on, you cannot see into the sky. It is a desert. When you relax, though, and see the sky all at once, then you see what is there: swallows, feeding in the evening, ever higher and higher above, in an infinite regression. ✦

*U*nlike the terns, swallows will occasionally light upon the earth. Like the Eagle landing craft touching down on the moon, they come down to the ground to gather mud for their nests. They settle around pools of water, like butterflies that sometimes cover the earth in colour, their wings beating slowly back and forth, like fluttering bed covers under which people move slowly, making love. The sun streams in through the windows.

On some mornings in May, when the sunlight is the colour of Saturn on a winter night and drifts in clouds like pollen, a steady stream of swallows glides down from under the northern eaves of my house to the pools of water around the leaking connections of my water hoses. As I plant my onions and carrots and beets in the light-coloured clay of the Plateau, my fingertips are rough and dark with soil and small stones, and every touch is intensified. Every grain and pebble of the world brushes against me. Sometimes the light is so thick and moves in such bright, streaming eddies that it obscures all the world—all of it, that is, except for small rivers of birds around the water hose, balling up small lumps of mud the size of peas and carrying them up one at a time to the eaves. They keep it up for an hour, then scatter off together to feed. And there, high up, drenched in the white light that blows above the crowns of the pines, the swallows grow infinitely small, until they disappear. The next day, they are back, and the next, and the next, until, after two weeks, the nests are finished, each one with a bird's head staring inquisitively out. ✈

The swallows are even more inquisitive than the cats. When the swallows first come back from a winter in California, the cats run from bedroom window to bedroom window along the north side of the house, knocking down plants and ornaments, trying to reach up and through the glass at the top corners of the windows, tails swishing frantically, then leaping down and trying another window. It's pretty destructive. By the next day, they have calmed down somewhat, and are sitting on the balcony railing, craning their necks around the side of the house to watch the swallows a metre away. Well, they may be a metre-stick away, but they are also completely unreachable. Damn.

After a few more days, the cats don't pay the swallows any attention. They lie on the bed while the shadows of swallows swoop and dive over them, and don't even stir. When I draw up the blinds on the windows to look out on the morning weather, the white blossoms of the strawberries and raspberries are like snow and the night clouds are beginning to break up. As soon as the blind goes up, the swallows in their nests at the edges of the windowframe crane their heads around to see what it is I am doing. They stare so intently, so full of assurance, and so without guile of any kind, it is as if I, too, had a nest under the eaves.

As we lie in bed on other mornings, the yellow light of morning comes in, diffused through the blinds, casting no shadows except the shadows of the swallows cast against the blinds from outside. Projected into the room, the shadows wheel across us and then gain speed suddenly across the right angle to the wall, the ceiling, the dresser, the mirror, and pass through the walls, and then return. For hours. Sometimes the shadows of twenty birds flit over us as we lie in the yellow light. For us, 7:00 AM is first thing in the morning. The air in the room is stale and hot. For the swallows, though, the sun has already been up for three hours. The day is theirs. ⋗

Swallow season is dandelion season. The lawns and grassy fields along the shore become seas of light. For six bright weeks, the dandelions are the only colour in a grey spring. Six weeks is a long time—as long as our entire summer here on the Plateau.

When I step out to pick dandelions to decorate a pancake covered with whipped cream and last year's strawberries, or to pick buckets of dandelions to boil on the stove with oranges and honey to make wine, the roar of bumblebees in the raspberries floods the air and the swallows trapeze by overhead on their long strings.

With dandelion wine, there are no shortcuts: only the very ripest dandelions will do—the ones fully open, round, and dusted brightly with pollen. It takes an hour to fill a small bucket. My fingers come up yellow as saffron, like the fingers of a priest in a temple in India. I boil the dandelion wine again at first snowfall, with peaches and ginger and cinnamon, and the light of the flowers again fills the house. ⋗

It is early April. Bob is out next door, clutching an aluminum extension ladder and hammering the deck railing back onto his house. It's the same every year. You could set an atomic clock by it: every year Bob bangs away at the railing and every winter the snow and ice take their toll. For Bob, this is yard maintenance. He believes that the best thing to do with his lawn would be to pave the whole thing, maybe make it into a tennis court, a really big tennis court, with a house instead of a net. About once a year he brings the idea up over a beer. Then he goes under his deck to see if he can start the ride-on mower, which has sat there for six months. Every year, it's the same: the engine turns over and over, ever more slowly, until the battery won't turn it over at all anymore, then Bob goes inside. A week here or there is not pressing, as far as lawns and Bob are concerned. Grass grows. We all know that. Get over it.

Actually, in Bob's universe, there are only two civilized reasons for being outside. The first is to sip a gin and tonic or, if things have gone well in the basement, a dark homemade beer, while looking out at the lake. Well, not really. It's more like, he looks at what little of the lake he can see through the wall of my house: a glare of water to the left, a hint of reeds through the pines to the right. Actually, because of the dribbles of mud from the swallow nests that line the eaves, he can't even see the wall properly. The second reason is to get in some good barbecuing. Bob is a master at barbecuing. He should host his own TV cooking show. His ratings would go through the roof. Most barbecuing has to do with coals and heat. Not as far as Bob is concerned. No. Bob's technique requires smoke—the more smoke the better. Bob's hamburgers are not so much cooked as smoked. Smoke pours out of the machine, fills the porch, pools around the house, and flows down in a river into my garden and dissipates among the aspens in thin, blue clouds. All the while, Bob stands in the kitchen, watching the smoke approvingly through his screen door. From his place, it looks perfect. From my place, it looks like a reason to call the fire department. When Bob really gets going, a side of salmon is indistinguishable from a grass fire. It is a three-siren event. Once things settle down, though, and the smoke is flowing freely down off the side of the porch like one of those pictures of waterfalls taken on a slow shutter so that the water blurs like silk as it falls into glistening space, Bob's two pursuits can be easily combined. Quite comfortably, Bob alternates between smoke above the barbecue and drinks on the front deck, with a full view of the swallows and the source of their mud—my garden. Bob hates gardens, but the swallows have hit upon an essential truth: dig down anywhere in the Plateau, from Quesnel, two and a half hours to the north, to Clinton, an hour to the south, and you will strike clay. It's great for the swallows, but tough for my carrots. It's great for Bob, though. Bob makes superb hamburgers but hates carrots. Besides, a look out over the lake while the hamburgers are smoking can easily be combined with watching me attack my chickweed and birdweed and lambsquarters and pigweed and ragweed and couchgrass and shepherd's purse and wireweed and God knows what else that loves clay that much.

You see, Bob loves to give advice. Bob's salmon is worth a two-hour drive, but he hates to see a man use a shovel, and is really down on vegetables, especially carrots. For Bob, there is something satanic about carrots. It doesn't matter that his wife, Barb, loves carrots, or that for years now I've planted extra rows of carrots for her. Bob has to watch the damn things grow, wasting perfectly good ground for a tennis court. Barb could sit down and eat them by the bucketful. Not Bob. For Bob, carrots are just the worst of a bad situation. In fact, for Bob the whole business of gardening is a form of insanity to be approached only from a respectful distance, and for that you need a good solid railing, to lean on while sipping a good solid drink. You have to steady yourself.

So, to see Bob out hammering, and on a ladder, is a real event in the neighbourhood. It happens only one day a year, like the day the loon returns to the lake, or the day the swans come by, or the day in July that Al, my neighbour on the other side, starts tuning up his snowmobile, getting ready for the big morning when the snow comes down. Bob's hammer-and-ladder day effectively doubles his vocabulary of outdoor activities in one fell swoop—like baking a plum pudding for Christmas *and* serving fruitcake.

This year, though, it's different. After a half hour of slipping aside the bedroom blinds, peering out past the swallows peering in to see what I am peering out at, I finally see what Bob has done. There above the broad sheets of plate glass, framing his high, vaulted living room, Bob has built a little wooden ledge, and on this ledge he has installed an owl. It is a truly beautiful owl of moulded plastic painted brown and white. It looks like a little garden gnome up there. It looks totemic. Who would have known? →

$\mathcal{N}$ow, I let the swallows make their nest on my wall because they eat two-and-a-half times their weight in mosquitoes every day, and I really appreciate that. The downside is that for most of the year my house looks like a painting by Jackson Pollock—an industrial spill spewing for forty kilometres down the 401 in Toronto. The dogwood bushes lining the house are twisted and blighted with the effluent from my swallows. Just think: I rescued the dogwoods from the spring depredations of moose in the 110 Mile swamps for this. I figured that any bush that could survive that kind of environment would do just fine in the wet of my yard in the spring, where every shovel hole turns into a well.

The swallow poop, in white and black streaks, ammoniac, is another matter. I do like living without mosquitoes, though, so I put up with it. I also know very well that the only reason I can afford this luxury is that my house is sided with vinyl. In late September, when the beans and petunias have collapsed in black mounds of stringy pulp, when the yellow leaves steam off the aspens like moths slowly beating their wings, scattering lightly as they strike the soil, I get out my ladder and foot by foot scrub the wall of my house. The swallow houses stand empty above me under the eaves, like the Anasazi cliff dwellings in Arizona and New Mexico. One touch of spray from my hose and they soften and fall. After three hours the house is clean and sparkling, my arms ache, and my hands are numb in the cold. A few crows fly overhead laughing. They find most things funny. I think they're in on it with Bob. ⟩

Bob doesn't have it so lucky. His house is sided with cedar. You can't scrub that stuff. He has obviously resorted to desperate measures. Last summer, and the summer before, the swallows nested twenty feet above Bob's deck, at the gable of his house, and transformed the big plate glass window in his living room into a whitewashed latrine. A pile of swallow guano three inches thick built up on the deck right in front of the sliding glass door into Bob and Barb's dining room. Bob had obviously had enough. You can mess with Bob's yard, but don't mess with his enjoyment while he watches the cooking shows on TV. Hence the owl. It looked like something out of Winnie the Pooh. I agreed with Bob. This was definitely going to do the trick.

It didn't bother the swallows in the least. In retrospect, it would seem that Bob and I have proven beyond a doubt that owls are not predators of swallows. We can say this with some certainty because the swallows went about their business, building mud nests and raising their young as if the owl wasn't even there.

After three years it still sits there proudly, watching out over the garden and the meadow leading down to the white swell of the lake, with a white crown of swallow guano. Dribbles of swallow disdain run down over its face. ⟩

The work of a landlord is never done. The first I knew that something was wrong was when seven-year-old Leandra began to cry uncontrollably. She had been staring out her bedroom window at the swallows nesting on the windowframe above it, dreaming of them snuggling down in their warm, little nests. One swallow had its head and wings out of the nest and was watching her, or so she thought, and she was watching it in turn. It was an intimate moment between girl and world. After fifteen minutes of this, though, the bird still had not moved. Leandra slipped off her chair and went to her mother, crying that she thought the swallow was dead. Diane had a look at the bird and agreed that, yes, it looked dead, like one of those straw and dyed chicken feather and bark birds you get in flower arrangements, held up by a little green piece of floral wire. Hearing the outcry, Anassa came running in, stared with her mother and sister out the window as well, and agreed, yes, the swallow was dead. The three of them were very agitated by this point, especially since another swallow kept flying up and trying to get into the nest. Diane and the girls came down to me crying and howling in turn, so I, too, trooped up to have a look.

"It's dead," I said, peering along with them, four of us all in a row.

"You have to get it out," said Diane. "There are babies in the nest." She told me about the other swallow trying to get in and having to fly away. "It looks upset," she said. As if on cue, the bird fluttered up to the nest, then flew away, then tried again, its wings in a whirl, then left, screeching in its thin voice. "You have to do something," Diane said. "Now. They've been like that all night."

I got my ladder from where it hung on the fence behind a screen of wild rose bushes. My lack of enthusiasm was pretty obvious. Scratched and stinging, and with rose spines working in through my jeans into my leg, I set the ladder up against the house. The base of it vanished in a flood of ammoniac dogwood leaves. I brushed them aside. I was apprehensive. I was more than a little apprehensive. I was plain scared. When I was nineteen and working in the vineyards in the Similkameen, I used to hike up the cliffs above the farms, looking for chunks of soapstone. There was lots of soapstone, all right—just no good pieces that you didn't need dynamite to get at. Up in one of those dry arroyos, red-tailed hawks had dived upon me as I came close to their nest. It was four metres above me as I scrambled along the side of a five-metre cliff to get past a sheer piece of basalt that blocked my way out of the wash. When I was eighteen, it had been hummingbirds in the Okanagan, protecting their nest in a big, old ponderosa pine surrounded by sweet peas, just over the hill from Nazis who, people had warned me, had rigged up shotguns and trip wires to keep inquisitive crooks out of their attic windows. There, where the clay cliff fell away and the lake rose up to meet the sky as I plodded down to the lake through a skiff of fine, white dust, the hummingbirds dove on me, screeching like dive bombers. I figured the swallows would do the same to me up there on my old orchard ladder. I wasn't looking forward to this. ⇥

The swallows were a little apprehensive, too. As soon as I banged the ladder up against the wall, they began whirling in the air. The cat got in the act by prowling round the yard, swishing his tail. Bob watched silently through the black glass of his front room, the TV flickering in a corner. I grabbed my courage by the neck, pulled a hood over my head, slipped on a pair of heavy leather gloves, and climbed the ladder quickly, hoping to minimize my exposure to attack. By the time I got to the top, the swallows were frantic. There I was, level with Leandra's face, Anassa's face, and Diane's face, watching me in a row through the glass of the window. The window was reflecting Bob's house behind me, and the swooping bodies of the whole colony of swallows above the garden between us. With those heavy gloves on, it was like trying to pull the fuel core out of a reactor at Hanford, controlling the robot arms from a distance—too much distance. My hands did not feel like my own.

Clumsily, I did what I could. My nerves sang with the fear that I would botch the whole thing, and with an audience, too—an audience prone to tears, might I add. Unlike the audience, I had scrubbed that wall a few times with a plastic brush and a hose. I knew how fragile these nests really were. I was afraid of breaking the whole nest open and spilling nest and babies all over the shit-stained dogwoods below. There was nothing for it, though. I grasped the dead swallow lightly by her copper-coloured shoulders. She was stuck! Now I was really worried that I would tear off the whole front of the nest. I tugged gently this way and that for a few minutes, until I finally freed her legs and pulled her out. I peered into the dark opening of the nest, but I could see no young, and they were certainly making no noise. I climbed down the ladder, like a Secwepemc shaman into a pit house, laid the bird on the grass, and lowered the ladder down beside her so the other swallows could rest easy. They were still flying frantically above the garden. All the swallows that usually rise up above the house at great height and range out over the lake had been drawn down, until there were twenty-five swallows whirling just feet above my newly seeded peas.

Shadows flitted over me as I examined the swallow on the grass. The smell of the swallow nest clung to me as I picked the bird up again: a musty smell, not pleasant, almost acidic. By this time I had a cat twining around my legs, the girls watching through the black mirror of the window, with swallows dancing over their faces, and Bob out on the deck behind me catching a little morning sun with a cup of coffee.

The swallow's legs were chewed raw—there was virtually no meat on her thighs at all, and she had been glued to the walls of the nest by a crust of dried blood.

Whether that was an act of cannibalism on behalf of her children, or whether it was cat damage, I don't know. The grey cat looked guilty, but then he's a murderer and should look guilty. He has a lot on his shoulders. He is a dispatcher of souls. I fear they will all wait for him when he dies. I think he will try to play innocent. He's been practicing that look. ⸱

Don't fall for it. He is not innocent. Just the week before he had caught a swallow in midair as it swooped through the open-walled deck off of the kitchen—a masterstroke, I'll grant him that. Most swallows wouldn't be caught anywhere near such an enclosed space. They come straight at the house off the lake, and just before they are going to hit the glass of the windows swoop straight up and over the roof, at full speed. Not all of them, though. In the previous weeks, a few of them had taken to teasing the cat, and the cat was furious. He would stand on the deck railing, staring at the swallows in their nest, a metre away. With great curiosity and no sense of alarm they would stare back, two trim, white-capped heads peering out of the narrow nest-opening. No matter how the cat balanced above the emptiness and stretched one arm gingerly forward, he just could not get them. His tail would twitch and Bob would watch, laughing, from across the yard. In the process, the cat, unused to making any noise in his life, learned to make his first sounds: yaps of anger and frustration. What cheek. I should have washed his mouth out with soap.

The swallows seemed to be in on it with Bob and took it all in great sport. Instead of flying over the house to get to the sheltered north side where they had glued their nests between the upper window ledges and the soffits, they darted through the covered deck, just a foot above the cat's head. They relied on surprise and speed to see them through, dipping their wings tauntingly and bobbing with the *Tonight Show* good humour of it all as they passed over him. They didn't reckon on him being a murderer, however.

And so it came to pass that when I opened the kitchen door at 7:00 AM one morning, in addition to the decapitated and disembowelled mice and shrews and voles, there were the tiny drumsticks and head of a swallow. Murderer: 1. Swallows: Love. ✦

That particular nest stood empty the whole summer, as a grim reminder. For whom, I don't know. It didn't stop other swallows from taking their suicidal shortcut. All summer long they swooped through that porch, for a lark. They are birds so used to mastery and freedom in the air that they don't even suspect predators. In fact, they don't *have* predators. Or didn't.

Late in July I saw the cat spring up almost a metre from a sleeping position on the deck floor and just miss hooking another swallow with his claws. Thankfully, he never did, although it sure wasn't for lack of trying. The rest of the swallows were able to raise their young without any further bad luck. As for myself, I still don't trust a sleeping cat. ✦

I looked out front one day and the cat was perched on the porch railing five metres above the ground, leaning out over open space, agitated. So I went out on the deck in the wind and put my cheek against the cat's whiskers and looked where the cat was looking, and there, perched on the roof a metre away—just his head leaning over the aluminum gutter—was a crow looking back at me. ✦

Crows rule. One afternoon when Leandra was five, I took the girls to the beach. As we baked in the sun and the air swam around us like flames licking in a fire, a dozen crows tumbled into a fir tree just off the water and started yelling at the top of their lungs, looking, and sounding, for all the world as if they were at a Grateful Dead concert. One of them had a ten-inch-long stick and was banging it against a branch over and over and over. He needed a drum set in the basement and a few private lessons. He needed a soundproof ceiling.

I lay back on the hot, grey sand reading Italo Calvino's *Invisible Cities,* fifty-four portraits of Venice as an imaginary city—hanging from the clouds, made into an elaborate game of cat's cradle in the desert. All of them were more real than Venice's lagoons and drowning tides could ever be because it was a purer portrait of the mind—and of the heart. The sun was burning in the white pages while the girls played with the algae that had drifted into shore. They scooped up great, green globs of it, like something out of a 1950s comic about radioactive turtles/snakes/crabs (pick one), the misbegotten spawn of mad nuclear experiments lumbering ashore and terrorizing innocent villagers in their wood and paper houses. The stuff was gross. I couldn't watch.

The crow was not so easy to ignore: bang! bang! bang! bang! "Well, at least the bastard has rhythm," I thought to myself, lifting my eyes from the burning white book to a world that had become the negative of the world, "you have to give him that much." Black and white had reversed. I could hardly see a thing.

Bang! Bang! I couldn't keep my mind on the words at all, so I watched the crows instead, with a finger stuck between two opposing versions of Venice to keep my place. At first I thought the crows were up to something clever and sophisticated, but it sure didn't look very profound, and it didn't look like it was going to evolve into anything sophisticated, either. Actually, as far as I could figure, they were up to nothing at all whatsoever. They were just having a party. So I opened my book, as a green sea princess came to me out of the lake, green hair hanging down over her face, with green veils of slime trailing down from her hands in place of fingers, and giggling. I stared into the glare. ⇥

Those barn swallows under my eaves aren't the only swallows around. There are tree martins, too: purple-backed, sleek, white-headed, with long frock coats, looking like footmen on Catherine the Great's gilded coach. They used to nest out in a cluster of crippled and twisted aspens up the road. They were old trees, rotten to the core, their white trunks scarred and black—heaven to a tree martin. Same for the woodpeckers. They work their way around them every spring searching for bugs under the bark, smashing them out with their beaks. It's a strange kind of apparatus, you've got to admit that—as if instead of a lantern a coal miner had strapped his jackhammer to his head. The best time for this kind of work is around 5:30 AM. You lie in bed and hear your blood pounding in your ears like artillery. It makes for violent dreams.

For a while, the martins lived in one of those trees. When they had a few moments to themselves, they perched on the power wires outside the tree, under the red glow of the signal light on the transformer. I always thought that those little red lights were an indication that the unit needed servicing, or was drawing too heavy a load. Apparently not. That one has been burning for nine years. You could guide aircraft in by it. The martins thought of it as a porch light. ⇥

My house was of no interest to martins until one late-September storm surging in from the southeast hurled most of the junk I had piled up behind my garden shed across the yard: the kids' plastic swimming pool took off like a UFO and wound up out in the trees; tarps and sheets of plastic were wrapped around the pines on the front lawn; branches snapped off the fir down by the lake; and the aspens streamed, mint-green, as if in terror. Water pouring off the gutters hit the plywood deck with a sound like a hundred barrels, each containing one of a hundred stuntmen, banging off a hundred rocks at Niagara Falls. The storm also tore an eight-foot strip of fascia off the back of my house. I found it lying in the middle of my carrot patch the next morning. Of course, it had come from the highest, most difficult to reach part of the house, eight metres above the ground.

"You're not going up there," said Diane when I led her outside by the hand and showed it to her. "Hire someone, please."

The man I called did not come. He kept promising to come, but before he came the snow came. It was no longer safe to attempt it, and it was certainly too cold to go mucking around with a chunk of bent aluminum eight metres above the ground. I shrugged. From October to March it was going to stay like that. Oh well, it kind of helped my house fit in with the Cariboo style: blue plastic tarps for roofs, fibreboard, weeds growing up through dead pyramid cedars.

Come March, I phoned again, and again the carpenter promised to come. This time, though, the martins beat him to it. They came in April, when the ice tipped and slid into the lake like a glowing green Titanic, dissolving like a throat lozenge in the deeps. The martins arrived in the afternoon. Before I got out of bed the next morning, they were already hauling grass into the attic to build a nest. They slipped in under a flap of shingle, through a crack scarcely the width of a thumb. One day a strip of plastic from the sheathing of a bundle of lumber—a pretty common piece of plastic in these parts—dangled out of the crack and flew like a flag of victory over a castle battlement at Crecy in 1310. By the end of the day, though, the martins managed to drag it in as well.

I phoned the carpenter again and said, "Don't bother coming until September." ⇢

*A*ll through the summer the martins flew in and out over the bare wood. They had made it into their own little home on the range. The male spent hours every day sitting on the clothesline a little over a yard away from the deck railing, as if he didn't have a care in the world, and the cat squatted on the railing in groans of frustration. Even if I came and clapped my hands behind him, he would not take his eyes off the bird.

Me neither. I had visions of the martins flying freely through the attic, making a mess in the insulation the way the barn swallows did with Bob's front window. I thought of how much it would stink. I thought of how the whole house would soon stink. I thought of crawling up there through the entrance hole in the bedroom closet, past my wedding suit and Diane's spare pairs of shoes, and hauling down all that rotten insulation. It was not a good thought.

A better vision was the thought of these graceful birds flitting through that warm, wooden space. It made me feel as if the house was alive, as if it was giving birth. It had become more than shelter for me and my family: it had become Noah's ark.

I was worried about the mess, though, and resolved to have the fascia board replaced in September, once the world had stilled from the whirling, aerial world of the swallows, back to its slower, pedantic, human manifestation. Again I phoned, again the carpenter promised to come, and again he didn't. By this time, it had become a matter of principle.

˙ "I'll have to do it myself," I said to Diane.

"You will do no such thing," said Diane. She paused for effect. It was a long pause. A lot of effect. "What if you fall?"

By this time I had pretty well figured out that the carpenter's wife was saying pretty well the same thing to him. ✣

*A*gain the house breasted a winter beaming its weathered smile out to the neighbourhood. It was always the first thing I saw as I drove down the hill into the yard. I felt that everyone else felt the same way: Harold's Eyesore.

The next spring, I was getting demoralized, and didn't call early enough. There was no chance of getting the work done: this time the martins beat me to my phone call, let alone beating the carpenter. I gave up—except for one thing. Armed with a flashlight, I pushed aside the clothes in the closet and slithered my way up over Diane's wedding dress. I surfed through mounds of pink insulation. I balanced on the beams, amid the electrical wires, and tottered out to the gable. I shone the flashlight crazily on the trusses and the roof, studded with the tips of shingle nails shining like stars, but I saw no nest anywhere: no nest, and no mess. That was the really important part.

I was relieved. The attic smelled of pink fibreglass insulation. Nothing else. I balanced and ducked and swung under the strut to the gable, scraping my head on the nails. There was no nest there either. I had expected it to be somewhere in the open cavern of the room, with martins weaving in and out of the struts like I had done with a ribbon at the maypole ceremony in Cawston when I was a boy, dancing in and out among the girls. No such luck. ✣

*W*hen I peered over the end beam, though, with my neck bent back awkwardly and the wood pressing up against my chin, I could see the nest easily. It was a tidy little grassy affair above the soffits, only the breadth of a spread hand in from the edge of the roof with its doorflap of shingle. It wasn't like the nests of the barn swallows with their globs of mud. It had been lived in for three years, but it looked like it had been put up only yesterday. It was fresh and clean. I couldn't reach it to take it down, though, so I traced my footsteps back over the rafters. It was so crowded in there and since the pink insulation covered up the beams underfoot, it was exactly like walking through deep snow— except this snow was made out of cotton candy. Still, spun sugar or not, I had to make sure I stepped exactly where I had done before—like a cat. This wasn't walking. It was choreography.

After I had gathered a few more scratches on the top of my head, I slipped down through the hole into the closet, pulled the pink fibreglass insulation closed behind me—not unlike the shingle flap of those martins, actually—and dusted myself off. Then I hung Diane's wedding dress and my wedding suit and dress shirts and Diane's dresses back up on the rack and turned out the light. ⟡

That was two years ago. Last year, the martins wasted no time making themselves comfortable—and I mean comfortable. For a couple days, the house was an old brownstone in a Greek neighbourhood in Toronto, with everyone sitting out on their small front porches for the sweltering summer evening, watching the shadows from the Ontario Hydro transmission lines slowly cross the street until they faded into the dark and then watching them rise up again in the streetlights. For a few days the pair of martins perched on the clothesline like a pair of teens with glasses of lemonade on a porch swing, chatting about the weather, making plans for the future, maybe, but perhaps also just being the weather, and being the future. After a couple days of that, the female disappeared into her nest. The male was left out there on the blue wire that stretched from the roof to the pine tree, alone. He took the opportunity to preen himself. His feathers glinted in the sunlight. He spent a lot of time out there. Damn it, but he looked good.

At least, I thought so. The murderer was taking it very personally that year, though. He spent entire days out on the railing, yapping—yes, yapping—at the bird. He had completely lost any sense of decorum. Sometimes I think he should have been a dog. →

*A*fter the young were hatched, the male martin began running a very busy grocery delivery service, bringing the kids food, and every time he swooped in from the aspens, or out again from his shingle-flap, the murderer leaned way out on the railing to watch him fly in or out. The murderer was just barely hanging on—his whole centre of gravity was right over the open air and the grass waiting below. This cat's nerves were on edge. His muscles were tensed. He was losing weight. The birds had invaded his house. I guess it was like finding a cockroach in the bathroom sink or a mouse splashing around in the bag of oatmeal in the pantry cupboard. I was trying to be sympathetic. I imagined that the way the birds appeared and disappeared through the hole under the shingles was like having a hornet fly down the neck of your shirt and sting you four times before you could swat it dead and everyone laughed at the way you were jumping about, screaming and hitting yourself hard. Then you would swell up. Being genetically programmed to watch for things—like mice—that disappeared into holes, the cat went mad, that's all. He needed a straightjacket. He needed sedation. The cat had learned the pain of consciousness and thought. He had become human. It was pretty sad. The cat only came into the house for a few minutes at a time, then rushed back out to take up his place again on the railing. He hardly ate a thing for weeks. I thought that was about as bad as it could get for any one cat, but I was wrong, for in July the mother martin came out with the young, two martins three-quarters the size of their parents. The cat lost it. The day before, he had been obsessed with one martin sunning himself above the green lawn. Now there were four. The dismay on the cat's face was almost audible. While I was busting at the buttons like any proud new grandfather, he yapped and twitched with frustration. Fortunately for his heart, three days later the martins left and he could concentrate his loving attention again on the swallows. He wouldn't need nitroglycerine, after all. He wouldn't need bed rest.

I phoned the carpenter again. Again he promised.

I waited months for him to come.

Eight months later, the martins came back. ⤖

Out at Gustafsen Lake, martins live a wilder life in the old aspens. Out in those white trees covered with lumps of coal and blushings of soot, they fly like angels out of Dante, winging straight at the black knotted trunks and disappearing inside without slowing down—as if they are entering another world. When I saw them, we were sitting around an old campfire on the shore of the lake. The girls poked at a broken horseshoe in the hot grass, which spilled with ants and burnt tin cans that had turned to leaf-thin shells of rust. All around us, martins were plunging into trees and materializing out of them again. Above us, the aspen crowns were a shimmering mantle of green leaves mixing with white leaves, brilliant with sun, tossing. We were inside a dream. Lily pads floated on the green water. The white towers of cloud that lined the hills to the southwest were reflected among them, and as the sun had entered the clouds, both the lake and the old Gustafsen homestead were framed by a flare of silver fire. We were furiously swatting mosquitoes as we ate chocolate and dried fruit, dodging the yellow jackets that had suddenly found us with our hands full. The sky was bright blue and so thin that the darkness of space could be seen directly through its colour.

As they grew used to our presence, mountain bluebirds began to dart from tree to tree, bluer than the sky. For the first time I saw how their colour was camouflage. As I watched, one bluebird lit on a black poplar twig. The sun was rustling in the leaves, the golden grasses lining the north shore of the lake swished in a slow, steady, streaming wind pushing out of the lake onto the land. Framed instantly there by the towering blue sky, the bluebird vanished. Its camouflage was centred in the sky—obvious, visible, flaming, a brushful of blue. Angels would, I think, be like that. →

$\mathcal{R}$ecent history at Gustafsen Lake has been anything but centred. Only a year prior to our visit, it had been the scene of the largest police operation in BC history. The RCMP and the army were patrolling the bush day and night to contain a group of natives who were determined to occupy the land. The local band at Canim Lake didn't want them to occupy the land. Lyle James, the rancher who owned the property, didn't want them to occupy the land. Some of James's men had even tried to scare the campers away, riding into their camp on range horses and trying to smash it up. The fisheries officers who were shot at while driving by probably didn't much care if the natives stayed there, just as long as *they* didn't have to. And so it went. What had started as a sundance ritual had become a struggle for traditional land use. It had become a civil war. The RCMP did their job admirably, completely isolating the campers while at the same time remaining very visible on national TV, from the comfortable distance of 100 Mile House, an hour to the east on a network of logging roads. Cut off from town, from information, from food, and worst of all, from any supply of mosquito dope, the sundancers were jailed, the media moved on, and the martins still flew in and out of the trees, the sun still streamed out of the west, driven on the wind, and the bluebirds still danced as if they were words in a sentence spoken deep in the mind.

When we got there, the light still shone at Gustafsen Lake and the mosquitoes filled the air, while just down the road, at Boar Lake, big, burly men wearing military camouflage gear hurtled around on ATV vehicles, as if it was hunting season.

It was not.

During our first spring on the Plateau, the girls and I clambered up the cutbank of the highway and dug up poplars—slow, wooden drift from old, black-cankered trees. The flowers beneath their mothers and sisters were trodden down by cattle, and the fallen trees among them were rubbed bare by the new steers. As I threw the trees down into the high grass of the ditch, the girls hit each other and the standing trees with sticks and peeled the fresh green bark off the broken twigs as diesels thundered past. It was evening then, a short outing before dinner that became a torment of keeping the girls off the road—lured there by the agates among the gravel of the soft shoulder.

The next morning, the light was scented with saffron. The poplars had unfolded tiny leaves, drinking the water out of the muck of the backyard. In the branches of one of those chest-high trees sat a western bluebird, wearing a Venetian mask, the blue pollen of the flowers of the sky splashed over his back and breast. The bird flitted off as suddenly as it came and vanished almost immediately into the air.

Occasionally in the yellow light of the next few mornings—early, when the light itself was a form of the stillness within the air—I saw the bluebird again, sitting on a thistle or flitting among the black aspen trunks.

It was maddening. The trees were like the bars in an optical illusion printed in the back of a comic book, a pattern perfectly designed to deflect the attention. In the glare of white light I just couldn't focus between the trunks. Each one was so strongly outlined in the glare of its contrast that it was impossible to pick out tree or grass, or even rose bushes in pink flame. The rich scent off the roses filled the air until it was a memory of years of summers. It was sap distilled to a purity of essence. The light was a wave suspended in the air. The bluebird flew through it, dipping with each wingbeat, a fast flash, then gone—into the heartwood of a tree. ✧

In July, when the carrots glowed in the garden, each one like a green feather sprouting from the soil, and the aspen saplings were silver-barked and their leaves were like a dancer's earrings, the bluebirds materialized again. The mother was brown, with blue flight feathers; the young birds had just the faintest dusting of blue at the bases of their tails; and the father was as bright as a sky scribbled in with a child's sky-blue Laurentian pencil crayon. Four hours later they flew south. ✧✧✧

Jokers

One beats the bush and another takes the bird.
→English Proverb

This April, I walked into the black scrub out back, trying to shake off the grey thoughts of six months of leaflessness. The snow on the horse trails was spotty, gone completely to loose crystals of ice. It looked like mounds of wet, crushed glass spread out between the stumps.

The ravens hang around out there in the crowded, black trunks. It is a brooding and lifeless forest, scrubby and draped with black lichen between the stumps of the Douglas firs that formed the original stand. The stumps are rotten and glow red in the shadowy light. Their butts are six feet thick at the ground.

As I ploughed through the eight-inch snow, following a deer trail down to Walker Valley, one big raven flew in large, sweeping circles overhead, keeping her eye on me. Walker Valley is a long string of marshes and aspen grasslands, part of the chain of shallow depressions leading west from the Cariboo Mountains of Wells Grey Park, through the town of 100 Mile House, north to the San Jose River Valley and Williams Lake, and down to the Fraser River at Soda Creek. At its closest, Walker Valley is three kilometres from my house. Its ponds have been dredged to provide duck habitat, with dams to control the water flow. All summer they are crowded with ducks and geese. The gravel of the dams at the lower end of each lake is carpeted with red plastic shotgun shells.

In the tall marshy grass on a point jutting out into one of the Walker Valley ponds that day, a coyote was pouncing on mice, his four feet bounding in unison, his back arched, his whole face and all his attention focused into his leaps. Again and again he punched into the grass. I hung back for ten minutes, watching him. Once he stopped and watched me back, then turned easily away and continued at his work. When a wind began blowing through my thin sweater, the first sign of a coming storm, I figured I had fifteen minutes to find shelter. Having convinced myself that the coyote was comfortable enough with me that I wouldn't disturb him, I tried to slip past to the left, but as soon as I had taken five steps he turned and loped effortlessly up the slope—on just the trail I had picked out. As I followed him up in my gumboots, he quickly vanished among the trees.

The trail pulled me up through dust to mud and then to white, grainy snow. When I hit the melt line halfway up and my breath was coming hard from the climb, the hair stood up on the back of my neck. Standing still and cold, I slowly turned from the bleak valley and searched among the thick, crowded trunks of the trees. My eyes quickly locked on the eyes of the coyote, who was watching me. He was exactly the colour of the trees and the grass. When he moved away, he was the grass slipping among the grass—what had materialized from grass was returning to its original shape.

The heaviness of that late spring vanished in that moment. As I turned for one last glance over the white ponds strung out among the rushes and the litter of old beaver stumps below, clouds were rolling brown and purple to the north, like a giant grouse brooding above Lac La Hache, and I saw a flit of blue—a bluebird in a grove of poplars in a small draw running down the side of the hill towards the water—just a flash, then it was gone. ❧

When I took Leandra to the bus stop the next morning, we played an impromptu game of soccer with a lump of snow while we waited for the bus to trundle in. As we booted the snow around, and as it scattered and skittered, slid and splashed, the croak of a raven came from the firs across the road. I say *croak*, but it really was a sound like a hand rummaging in a kitchen drawer, looking for a potato masher. Another kitchen drawer answered from deeper among the trees. The calls floated easily through the air, like two old poplar branches scraping together in a wind, the hollow trunks amplifying the smallest noise into deep, tubular groans.

As Leandra and I checked each other in snow soccer, the ravens continued their conversation. Often our ball disintegrated at a really good kick—suddenly we would be chasing several balls, then just a scatter of snow, then one of us would kick a new lump of snow out of the bank. The ravens' conversation sounded like the CBC Morning News: the latest roadkill out on the highway, that cougar kill up by the bluff, a discussion of Hobbes' *Leviathan*, Rousseau's theory of the origin of language. As the bus drove away and Leandra waved from the window, I stood in a small blue cloud of carbon monoxide and burnt oil and looked up. The tops of the firs were swaying in a light wind, against a sky so bright it had vanished. Through it I caught just the shadow of a raven's presence, moving from tree to tree. ⇥

Ravens and bluebirds and coyotes aren't the only tricksters in this landscape. There are the horses of the 105, for one thing—or a dozen things. And there are cows. Maybe it's something in the water.

The trickster cows live in Walker Valley. The day they found me there, visibility was about twenty feet. The birches along the fenceline trails were crystallized with hoarfrost—giant, frozen flakes like moths that had fluttered down from the stars and had folded their wings before dawn. When I came out of the trees, the fog was so thick I could scarcely see more than the clumps of grass immediately in front of me. My breath was freezing to my beard. I was becoming a snowman. Suddenly a huge shape loomed up in front of me: a bear! Damnit!

The fog swirled, and the shape revealed itself: a cow. She was staring back at me intently with deep, brown eyes. Oh man. I spoke to her gently through my pounding heart and stepped carefully forward. I heard cows all around me then, changing position as I changed mine. I couldn't see them, though. I had no idea what they were up to. My back prickled. When the fog finally cleared, I was standing in an old branding corral, surrounded by cows, ruddy brown and black. From wherever they stood, ten feet away or two hundred yards up on the shoulder of a hill, their heads were all turned towards me, and I was in that hated thing. Not one of them was moving. It was a game of freeze tag.

I slowly picked my way through those cows. They breathed fog, but they did not move—until I passed. Then they closed ranks behind me and slowly, measuredly, followed. I felt like I do when I'm driving down the highway and a big semi comes up and crowds my tail to push me on. Honk!

Every time I turned around, the cows froze again. They milled behind me at a distance until I climbed back up the hill and was swallowed once more by the clouds. ✸

Every morning the crows fly into town to work. It's a good ten kilometres into 100 Mile House as the crow flies, ha ha, but they chose to live out of town, among the trees, despite the distance. I can't blame them for that—I've made the same decision. The living is easy out here.

Still, you have to get up early to see the crows. If you sleep in past

6:00 AM, you'll only see them on the job; but if you get up at 5:30, you'll see them when the fog lies low over the water and the loons' cries flow through it liquid and green. At that hour, Venus burns like a scrap of zinc above the southern hills and an early sun flares low on the horizon like a city in flames.

The crows roost in the big firs at the north end of the lake. In the mornings they make their way single file, sometimes in little family groupings of three or four, over the water and into 100 Mile. It is a quiet, steady flight, and you can see them putting energy into their wings to get themselves to town as quickly as possible. It takes the crows about a half hour to pass, like scraps of black carpet moving through the air.

The crows have several work sites. The dumpster behind the mall is one of their favourites. I have seen three or four crows sitting on top of the dumpster lid, a couple others on the ground, tearing at french fries and coleslaw and scraps of paper and cardboard, and a couple others flying in and out and throwing garbage onto the ground. Several dozen patrol the schoolyard—especially the bus-loading zone, where there is usually a good supply of dropped cookies, chips, and chocolate bar wrappers to worry over. Others patrol the field out back, and still others flutter up from the backs of pickups when you come near. ⟶

Sometimes the ravens join in. I've been stopped on the road in front of the school by a sea of crows as they milled around like one of the crowds standing on the bridges of Vancouver one summer evening to watch the fireworks displays shot up from boats in False Creek. In the midst of that crowd of black-suited and serious crows were three or four ravens, standing easily three times as high as the crows. I tell you, those ravens were giants among the pygmies. They could join the Harlem Crowns, come into town, and take *anyone* on, with one wing tied behind their team jackets. They stood almost motionless. They looked regal and imposing. They didn't pay me any attention at all. There was no getting through. I parked. ✧

After lunch hour, anyone looking out of the windows of the secondary school across town can see garbage sailing out of the mouths of the garbage cans lining the soccer field. It looks a bit as if the garbage cans have somehow slid down the spectrum of objects in this world and have become volcanoes. This eruption can go on in a steady, stuttering rhythm for five minutes or more. The whole time, all around each garbage can, crows strut, pecking at the paper, turning it over. It's like the social life of wolves: for a crow, hunting is pack behaviour. If one of them gets a hopeful piece, say a gravy-soaked paper french fry tray, it stands on it with its scaly twig-feet and rocks forward, tearing at it with its beak. Eventually, the crow will flap out of the can with a particularly tasty morsel, and another, or even two, will take its place, and perhaps one will even balance on the rim of the barrel, precariously, as if it were a wild teeter-totter. ✧

In the evenings, the crows return. They come back lazy and happy, in a sooty stream that takes a half hour to pass over the flare of the lake. At first, the crows are a scatter of specks across the south, flapping in and out of visibility; then they're a line of eager birds flying steadily forward, more or less in single file but many of them keeping pace with each other, even passing each other like horses on a track, neck and neck until one pulls ahead with a sudden burst of speed. Still others swing out wildly over the lake or the trees, hoping to outflank the leaders. Sometimes the stream of crows thins out into clumps, and just when you think they all have passed, suddenly others show up as specks to the south. All the time, the crows don't make a single noise—nothing, in fact, until they reach their perches for the night. Then they break out into a raucous chorus of cries and yells and guffaws. Some of the crows fly more slowly, with flight feathers missing from their wings; others are young, without the strength to keep up; others dip and dive and swoop and loop-de-loop, radiating sheer happiness and strange good humour; and all the time the light is fading. The bright clover yellow disappears. By the time the last crows pass by, only the lake and the sky are still shining in an already dimming world.

Every night, there is one crow that shows up almost five minutes later than the others, beating her wings hard, and hardly getting any purchase on the air, but eventually she passes as well, and settles in a roosting tree just as the raucous laughter rises to a crowing crescendo, and suddenly it is quiet and dark and I think of hundreds of black eyes looking out satisfied from their dark trees at the world, and in the land of the crows another day has passed and the eyes shut. ⇝

After years, I noticed this about crows: as they fly, their flight feathers are completely spread. I always thought they flew by flapping their wings, the way I did when I was a kid and ran around the farmyard, thrashing my arms up and down and cawing as the dog bounded around me, barking. I didn't even consider there might be different explanations; I always thought that crows used their strong shoulder muscles to raise and lower their wings—like arms. Well, I got that wrong. I got it right about the wings and the muscles raising and lowering them as they fly, Okay, but I misunderstood about the flying. The thing is, crows don't do it with their wings. They do it with their wing tips, where the feathers are splayed out like the fingers of an open hand. When crows fly they are balancing on their fingertips. It is a tightrope act. ⇝

I was tobogganing on New Year's Day with the girls on the 108 Ranch golf course, riding down the big old wooden toboggan I pulled years before out of the dump in Summerland at the end of a day bottling wine with Gord—some rescued family tragedy, I figure. Over and over again the girls and I took the jumps by the nineteenth hole, tore down the crazy straight stretches past the brightly snow-suited forms of other families—spread-eagled in the snow or trudging back up, pulling their sleds behind them—and blasted out past the aspens towards the third green, five hundred yards away in the foot-thick snow. I sat myself firmly up front to steer, with my feet tangled amongst the ropes under the toboggan's back-curled and wobbly tongue. The girls wiggled into place behind me. Hanging onto the ropes of the toboggan, launching off, tottering, feet splaying out for balance, we flew down that hill, soaring, flexing, and landing with a hard oomph, like dropping a crate of encyclopaedias on a hardwood floor. The snow flew up over our faces in a spray of ice. Half the time I closed my eyes as the ice spewed up over me like surf on the north pole of Mars. The girls screamed with delight. Usually I lost one of them about halfway down, and as she fell off she sent us careening off course into the deepest snow. The toboggan sailed across it with only a low scraping rustle, until we slowed and slowed and came to a stop and fell over sideways, the snow leaking down our necks.

Lying there after one of the trips, with the blue sky at a crazy angle above me, I saw the crows come, flying in close ranks from the forest behind the clubhouse, out over the greens (whites, actually) and ski trails, towards Sepa Lake. They were moving with a steady purpose. I raised a snow-covered arm and waved at my old friends and called out a greeting. One of the crows, as usual, was flying far behind the others, lolly-goggling, out-of-breath, just not worrying too much about this flock thing. She was getting along just fine.

No she wasn't. Not when you considered the hawk. It was coming in fast from the east, at ninety kilometres an hour, its wings folded back like a jackknife. I felt like an ancient Roman soothsayer, reading the flights of birds for auguries about the Emperor and the Senate, who was going to poison whom in what palace coup, which general, in the pocket of which senator, was going to march back on the city and restore order: a dangerous job, to be sure. It was best to have a personal food-taster. The space between hawk and lonesome crow narrowed very rapidly. The crow, God help her, was not looking in her rear-view mirrors. She didn't notice a thing.

When the hawk was six yards behind her, I thought the crow was going to be a goner for sure, but she wasn't. She saw the hawk at the last minute—actually, the last quarter second—dipped sideways and slid out of the way and backwards in a rough scramble, tumbling and giving up her grip on the air, and so saved herself: the hawk couldn't adjust his flight quickly enough to repeat all that—like a mirroring exercise in an improv act—and splashed right past her. He banked sharply and came back for her again, but the curve took away half his speed, and this time the crow was not alone. The other crows had heard her squawk; when the hawk came back for the straggler, he did so within a cloud of angry crows. They broke his angle of flight, pecked at his wings, darted in front of him, said some really bad things about his ancestry, and ruined his concentration. After three more tries, each one slower than the one before, the hawk flapped wearily off towards the trees.

The crows all reassembled, placed the straggler in the middle of the group, and continued on their way to Sepa Lake.

I continued to lie in the snow until Leandra pulled my hand.

"Come on!" she said, and we got up. ✢

Crows aren't easily fazed. You don't just leap out from behind the corner of the house and shout, "Boo!" and expect to see them scatter to the four winds. They probably wouldn't even raise an eyebrow, actually. The most you might reasonably expect would be for them to hop a few feet sideways and continue digging up your newly seeded peas, the organic ones, the ones without the pink fungicide coating. That pink stuff might look like caramel popcorn, but it tastes so bad. Crows have pride.

Respect, though—well, they don't have much of that. For moments of disrespect, I have just the thing: a scarecrow. His name is Chubby, and he is five years old. For a spine he has a six-foot long 2 x 2 and for a head an empty plastic milk jug, nailed firmly to the top of his spine with a two-and-a-half inch spike. His face is an old burlap sack that once even had an expression of smug contentment, painted on with a wide-tipped black felt pen. After five years of sun and rain and snow, though, the world has pretty well succeeded in wiping the smile completely off Chubby's face. He wears a red Bardahl cap and an old pink and tan checked shirt stuffed with a length of black plastic sheeting from a pallet of lumber. His jeans have huge holes in the knees and are bleached and faded by the sun and stiff from the rain. They, too, are stuffed with scraps of black plastic sheeting and are tied at his waist with a length of hemp twine. When he was new and I drove him in among the ten-foot-tall sunflowers, Chubby cut a pretty striking figure, albeit a portly one, but he doesn't look very imposing now. He has fallen over too many times in windstorms, face-first into the mud. To keep him on his feet, I finally lashed him to the end post of a raspberry trellis last fall. There he remains, cinched to the post with a loop of wire around his neck. Chubby has become a part of the scenery—even the red of his cap is so faded that it blends in with the muted colours of the spring garden.

The crows must think so, too. The other morning I found one of them, like a Tsimshian chief in all his ceremonial regalia, calmly and without expression—but with great curiosity—walking up and down the rows of onions I had just planted, plucking the onion sets from the ground and tossing them to the side. I don't have a clue what he was looking for—it couldn't have been onions: he didn't eat, or even try to eat, a single one of those. I went out and chased him away, waving my arms and yelling. It took me ten minutes to straighten out the onion patch, and, you know, I think he was doing it just for the joke of it. He had made me into a scarecrow. I gave Chubby a sour look. ⇌

I planted sunflowers. They grew like triffids. They grew as tall as I would be with Anassa sitting on my shoulders and Leandra sitting on hers—a kind of family totem pole. They had big white and black striped seeds that smelled like distilled petroleum on my fingers. It was a sharp smell, a volatile mix of the regular unleaded I buy down at the Tempo to get my car into town and back, the vinegar in which the Greeks soak their Kalamata olives, and a fifty dollar bottle of first-press Cabernet from Summerland. The sunflower leaves and seeds smell of petroleum, all right, sure, but not like petroleum distilled in a vast plant of storage tanks and metal piping in a suburb of Edmonton. Baking in the sun, the sunflowers make it out of the mountain soil itself. This stuff is homegrown.

All summer the sunflowers grew taller, and all through August the potatoes that found themselves more and more in their shade shrivelled and devoured their own tubers, like chicks feeding on their yolks inside their shells, until they just vanished in a few shrivelled black stalks, like toadstools in the spring that stink up the air with the sweet, rank perfume of a dead cat and then just as quickly vanish down to a black thread. Potato pancakes were going to be at a premium in the winter. Rats.

The sunflowers grew so tall, and took so long getting to those dizzying heights, that when they finally swelled out into seed heads they had used up the summer. There was no time left to slowly bend over and face the soil, to drop their seeds, returning to the earth the oil they had distilled from the sun: before they could manage it, the blackbirds came back. They came in groups of twenty-five as soon as the outer rim of seeds on the dinner plate-sized sunflower heads had set but were still soft and pliable. Within an hour the birds had pecked around the rim of each of forty flowers in a flurry of wings and happy chattering, seeds and seed shells flying all around them with abandon like a bunch of basketball players spitting Spitz out of the window of their bus, heading north from Prince George for a tournament in Fort St. John. The cats slipped across the yard in a fluid glide and lurked in the dogwoods like moray eels hissing at Jacques Cousteau from the Great Barrier Reef, but to no avail. The birds were as bright as angelfish in the sun and within a half hour they were gone as quickly as they came. The sunflowers were a mess.

It continued like that for a month, as the fall dragged on and on and it seemed as if the snow would never come. Every five days until the end of October, the blackbirds returned. The biggest male perched on one of the giant leaves on the tallest plant—a plant so pumped on nitrogen that it had not yet formed a head. From that height, he watched as the others ate their fill, husks flying and the happy sound of munching and dinner table conversation filling the garden. Chubby listened to it all, unshaken. He didn't lift a finger. By the time frost came, there were no seeds on the stalks at all, only the empty, seedless rings of husks directly in the centre of the flower heads, and the birds were gone.

One morning the leaves were black and hung off the stalks like scraps of soaked, oily rag in the back of a garage. It was winter and the ground had an iron crust. When I went to dig the last of the potatoes, my shovel sounded against the ground like an old church bell stuffed with cotton. Bonk. →

Crows always get the last laugh. To crows, we are the piñata at a child's birthday party, a bull brightly decked out in coloured paper scraps. The crows see themselves as the children with the stick, blindfolded and swinging wildly.

Sometimes they let us have the stick, to see if we know what to do with it. They first let me have a try twenty years ago in Victoria, when I was still dreaming of making the city back into the land. In springtime in Victoria, the crows stand high in the fretwork and arches and flying buttresses and among the golden tapers of bloom on the limbs of the horse chestnuts that line Cook Street. Their caws fall like rain over people passing below—sticky yellow chestnut rain. My friend, the poet Robin Skelton, wrote about those crows. He might have come from England, but he had a Bohemian past—even took the crow as his totem animal when he became a witch in 1970. It was a good choice. Those Victoria crows are pretty cheeky. They gather together there in the chestnuts, getting their nests ready for the year, sorting out their territories and relationships. It is *Peyton Place*. It is one too many seasons of *Friends*. Robin helped me find my way back to my land. The crows just poked me with a stick.

Literally. From their perches in the branches, the crows of Cook Street cock a head and, with a glint of a pebbly eye, drop a stick, or even an old chestnut, on people passing by underneath, then explode in guffaws. No one picks the sticks up. The laughter is taken up by crows in the surrounding trees, and then the street hushes as the crows wait for the next crow to drop sticks as a person passes beneath his branch, when they all break up over it all over again, hardly able to control themselves. Their bodies skitter with laughter. Their wings go completely rigid with it. They even play this trick on old, blue-haired ladies, and take just as much delight in that. The old ladies swat at the sticks and grow angry, which they display by walking more stiffly and more quickly.

In my years in Victoria I never could get angry at those crows. With the trees on fire with flowers and the green flames of their new leaves fanning in colourless smoke, I was always infected with good spirits. I looked up into the spreading cathedrals of the horse chestnut trees and saw a complete world, a vast volume of space filled in all directions with an intricacy of intermingling branches, and in them, staring directly back at me, the cocked head and the basalt eye of a crow, and for an instant there was no sky.

When Robin died in 1997, I went to Victoria for his service and read a poem about taking over his work, about his life continuing in the things of the world, about rain rising from the sea and falling in the mountains and the trees rising up to it. While local artistic dignitaries gave eulogies to Robin and his place in the artistic society in Victoria, the sun burned in through the plate glass, glaring and hot. Halfway through the formal eulogies—Robin's work with the art gallery, his years with the university, his support of the artists of Victoria—a crow walked in through the open French doors behind the speakers, through the pool of sunlight spilling across the parquet floor, strutted around, obviously keenly interested in the proceedings, then strolled out again. Robin's eldest daughter and two other members of her coven closed the service with a spell of release, ending it with the snuffing of a candle, and Robin was gone, into us and into the world, released from language into essence. Only a very few of us saw the crow.

And the crow saw us. ⇥

Sometimes we don't mind when the joke's on us. This is Dan's story, but it could be mine, too, because this is the story that we share. This is the story of finding wildness. Dan came to the wild earth with tackle in his hand, as a release from teaching chemistry in Nelson. I came to it with children on each hand and starlit nights. In the end, we both got there, or as close as it's possible to get. Dan's my brother-in-law, Danish on both sides of his family. He is tall, with clear eyes, a ready smile, and the easy assurance of a man who has found a durable balance between caring for people and the world they live in. When it comes to caring for himself, the Dane in him comes through: he goes inside himself; he chops wood; he goes fishing—small, intimate acts without grandeur or advertisement. Two thousand years of winter fogs breeds that into a family. As far as the fishing goes, the fish just aren't that important. What's important is the boat, the water, the mountains. What's important is being in the world. If the truth be told, Dan is allergic to fish. One brush of fish across his lips and Dan's throat swells up. Any more than that and he's finished for good. Dan's pretty big on catch-and-release.

Dan fishes the main arm of Kootenay Lake in an eighteen-foot boat he keeps in an old boathouse eight kilometres up the West Arm. I helped him lay the rails there—old, narrow-gauge salvage from a silver mine in the high alpine country above, the country where a decade and a half later Sasha Trudeau rode an avalanche down into the dark. Every time Dan fishes he winches the boat down by hand and, later, winches it back up again, as the ospreys glide past. They're all going for the same fish.

The main body of the lake is cold, fed by glacial water from the Purcells, high craggy peaks that see snow for eleven months of the year. The peaks and flanks of the range rise almost perpendicularly out of the lake in great blocks and tilted, up-thrust slabs. The lake is cold, deep, and nearly sterile, but in the depths there are big trout, up to sixty-five pounds, and because of them there are also a lot of boats, like Dan's. The big fish feed on kokanee, and as the kokanee population crashes—not many years ago, one hundred and fifty thousand fish washed up on the beaches along the West Arm—fewer and fewer of the big fish are caught every year. Dan is still trying, out there on the incessant, steel-grey chop of the main lake. When the kokanee population crashes, the ospreys listen to their stomachs growl.

One day, as Dan tells it, he was out trolling for luck with his thirteen-year-old son, when they noticed a lot of gulls, and even a few osprey—a good sign—feeding furiously at the mouth of a creek coming down cold and white into the lake south of Proctor. Water like that spills out blue and turquoise as it drops its glacial flour into the depths. You can see it for miles. Dan turned his boat southwest and rode over the chop, the bow of the boat smacking each wave as it crested it, like a rodeo rider slapping the thigh of a horse with his hat and yelling. That was one time, Dan says, that he didn't even get out his fishing tackle—because as he drifted in the chill wind, with the gulls screeching and diving at the water in a blur of white wings crossing in all directions, when there was a big fog of gulls all around him, he saw the big fish.

The gulls were rising out of the water with small kokanee in their mouths, even as others were diving in past them. Through the cloud of ascending and descending gulls, the osprey were coming in and lifting out again with larger fish, maybe fifteen inches long, buffeted by the gulls as they rose away. That's when Dan killed the motor on the boat, because all around him the big fish were rolling over on their sides on the surface of the water. They rose, scooped up kokanee in their big jaws, rolled, and dove again, over and over and over, massive, slow, moving with great power. Dan and his son watched them for half an hour, the boat lightly riding the swells. After twenty years of fishing the lake, hoping for one of the big fish, with fifteen thousand dollars of boat beneath him, that is as close as Dan's got yet, with the silver sky above him and clouds forming off the leeward edges of the peaks eight kilometres away, and behind them another range, indigo blue, and another, a pale pastel blush, blurring into the ridge of clouds that formed the horizon, and a fresh wind blowing over the lake, smelling even in the summer of snow.

It's pretty close. ⇢⇢⇢

Travellers

People live like birds in the woods:
When the time comes, each must take flight.
⇒Chinese Proverb

It was a week before our first Christmas in the Cariboo. After a prolonged fall of weeping rain and ochre grass, the weather had turned at last. For three days, snow had been drifting in sheets through the air. On the afternoon of the fourth day, the flakes were coming down as big as dandelions—so large that the crystal pattern of each flake was easily visible as it fell. Shovelling the driveway so Diane could get back in after work—her last afternoon before the holidays—I looked up into the flakes and lost my balance for a moment, caught between the movement of the flakes and their stillness, suspended above me in layers until they vanished in the heights of the sky twenty feet overhead. It was as if they were materializing out of the sky itself. They fell quickly, recreating themselves over and over again on my face and shoulders as they fell— until all the world was motion, streaming down—a motion upset by its abrupt cessation as the flakes struck the ground.

And there, as I scooped them up alongside the red dogwoods and threw them among the trunks of the crabapples lining the driveway, they achieved stillness. Space and time came together. The world hushed. Close overhead, two tundra swans glided past like stealth fighters, necks outstretched, as white as the snow. They flew in formation, wingtip to wingtip, without a sound and with scarcely a beat of their wings. I stood there with the snow melting on my eyelashes as the swans slowly swept away into the white air. Once again I was left with the streaming snow in the twenty feet of air between the white top of the air and the white ground. All the world had come to this one point, this one journey. ❧

When I saw the swans again, it was spring. We had closed up the house and gone out into the wind, bundled up in wool sweaters and toques and scarves. The girls were running ahead, laughing, tromping through the mud, seeing how deep they could get into the mud of the rangeland road and still get out again, and laughing even more when they couldn't. There were geese, Canada geese, ahead of them. The geese shied away when we came, honking, wings outstretched, sidling along parallel to the tracks. It wasn't helping them a lot to get any further away from us, and they were in a panic. These guys and gals had missed an important part of the Grade 10 math lesson on points and lines. Finally they grew so agitated that they darted across our path in single file and down to the water, honking, necks outstretched.

There on the ice in the middle of the pond were the swans. As we drew close—three hundred yards, no less—they lifted off and swung tightly together down over the black poplars to the next pond a kilometre away. It was like those National Geographic movies of the pelicans in Botswana or the flamingos of the Ngorongoro Crater: the swans reminded me that here, on the Plateau, it is the north that is my home, not the cities of the south, and it is the north that provides the markers and cycles of my year—the snow in my yard goes all the way to Siberia. The forces that drive my year are that first sunny day in May when in the space of a single afternoon the trees go from being leafless to fully leafed, drenched in yellow light; first snow, when in five minutes all the struggles of the year become inconsequential as we rush out to walk without a hat or gloves in the cold and then come in for a warm cup of dandelion wine mulled with peaches and ginger; and first swans, when the world is again full of hope after a long winter in a stilled world. ⇉

*A*fter eleven years on the Plateau, I've learned to trust my perceptions. The tattered Vs of sandhill cranes call from twelve thousand feet as they stream north to the Mackenzie Delta. Far below, I am hoeing the first shoots of dandelions from among my strawberries. Behind me a robin hops over the loose soil, one ear cocked, listening for worms. I raise my arm to the cranes and scan the sky, staring into the white glare of the sun. The sun blankets the whole stratosphere like sheet lightning that neither strikes nor rolls. High up, at the limit of what I am, I make out the thin black specks of the cranes: a ragged, constantly reforming stream moving at sixty kilometres per hour over the sprawling forests and clearcuts, following the big rivers north to spend their summer without darkness, fishing in the marshes on the Beaufort Sea.

The cranes return in the fall, when the air vibrates like a glass of red wine, a rounded mouthful of music in tones of copper and wool died with onionskins, chrysanthemums, and black currants. After the first frosts, the yellow leaves are streaming off the poplars so rapidly it seems they will never stop—as if in their shifting, musical rustle the tree is generating leaves as quickly as it casts them off. A thin skin of ice lays up in the bay, along and among the reeds.

The cranes pass overhead with their children this time, long skeins flying south, the sun glinting off them at that height, their calls dropping tattered through the fall wind—like poor radio reception in a mountain night. I lean on my hoe—still at it—to steady myself against the weightlessness of the sky, and stare up, even whirl around in the garden, my hand raised to my brow, until I see them—and through the music of the air that is instantly between us, fly off with them for the winter.

If I look deep in my memory, I see, year by year, cranes flying north and south like that. As a boy in the Similkameen Valley, they were flying up the crowded flyways from Mexico, long ribbons of birds above the windy orchards. As the sand whipped over me from the driveway and the blossoms of the apples drifted down like white flocks of seagulls settling on a windswept shore, the cranes passed overhead, high above the peaks of the back country. I travelled with them in my mind.

When the cranes fly overhead now, those days on the orchards come to me. Those years taste like apricot blossoms, thin and watery and infused with dandelions and yellow light and the smell of dormant oil gloving every tree with a dark, glistening, and pungent skin. When I hear the cries of the sandhill cranes today I am no longer standing in space, with evanescent gusts of time blowing over me, but am standing in time. It is a solid country. It is space that is a thin veil of cobwebs blowing in a cold October wind now, a thousand little tents of frost in the morning grass, vanishing as the day rises. ⁂

This spring, my father phoned from his orchard in Oliver, with news of the cranes. Up here on the Plateau the world was still frozen. There were eight inches of snow outside the thin skin of my windows. Down there in the Okanagan, though, the snow had already receded up the slopes, the wind was gusting and cold, and the soil was warm. Ants and the first bumblebees were flooding through the trees. As my father was planting new apple trees that morning, he had heard the birds.

"It was incredible, Harold," he said, in his rolling, German-accented English, clipping off the beginning and end of each word and rounding out the middles like globes of air floating up in a glass. "I have never seen so many. There must have been ten thousands birds passing in one hour. I looked up and saw a *V* above me, and then I noticed another *V*, and another and another. As far as I could see, the whole sky was full of birds, and it went on like that for an hour before they had all passed." For a moment I was there, standing at his side, tasting the lemon dust, cutting open pink peach buds to see which blossoms had frozen black at their cores and which had come through the winter cold. ⇥

The Okanagan is not a haven for birds, though. Granted, there are still massive clouds of starlings in the swampy hayfields of the old floodplains, rising out of the alfalfa when a car passes between the sagging fences and the broken spines of the haysheds, and among the pines along the hills blue jays still chatter and scold like ancient Aztec priests, and magpies still scrape dead rattlesnakes off the roads, yes. But songbird populations are low because of the orchard sprays, and robins, which nest among the cherry and apple trees, often lose their young to poison. Worst of all, the southern shore of Okanagan Lake north of Penticton has been filled in with boulders and crushed rock to make a freeway—the original shoreline now stands a hundred yards from water. The marshes there, at the foot of Okanagan Lake and the head of the Okanagan River—what must have once been the home of five thousand red-winged blackbirds—have been filled in to build a retirement complex, surrounded by tall, cinderblock walls. When the first phase of the project was undertaken in the early 1980s, the blackbirds moved to the bulrushes across the highway. When that swamp was filled in too, a decade later, a few blackbirds perched on bulrushes in the ditch, looking out, not over the swamp, but across a desert of gravel and concrete and clay, straight into the big graders and loaders. The next year, not a single bird returned, and with them disappeared the last sense of wildness in the Okanagan, the sense that the orchards were planted in a wilderness and the wilderness was giving fruit. Overnight, those orchards were planted in a complex of roads and streets. Only when I moved to the Plateau did I realize how much had been lost. The Plateau is alive with birds. They flood every part of the landscape. Moving here has been to move home. ⇥

On June nights I listen to a bittern. I have seen him only once, like a scrap of a willow stump among the reeds in the shallow water, his bill upthrust, frozen, blending in. He fills the night with a popping, booming noise, like a rusty hand waterpump sucking up air in a steady repetitive rhythm. He booms all evening, right into the dark. It's like the beat of a bass player in a jazz band, and the scream of an odd duck over it, as the air turns to water and it is night. All the ages of the world and all the nights of the world live in the air at once, within and expanding each other. ⇥

From a distance, the lake is carved from one luminous blue stone, but when you're out on it, it's black, shot through with a faint green, like the branches close to the trunks of forest trees. I have floated for hours on that water, in an old, red fibreglass canoe, its keel ground down from years of being dragged onto the shingle. I have spent hours watching the water drip off the end of my paddle, making lines of rings alongside the canoe, at first large, then increasingly smaller. By the time the smallest ones formed, and before I had dipped the paddle into the water again and pushed the canoe soundlessly forward, the ripples spreading from the first drops overtook the last. Deep in the black water of the lake white clouds floated, their light dimmed, as if they were shadows of themselves in an inverse world. They glowed below me, as if there was another world below me and it met mine at the film of water and light on which I floated. In the middle of the lake I was floating on air.

Suddenly twenty feet off the side of the canoe the loons have come, staring at me with their bright red eyes. They come up soundlessly, and float there for a few minutes before diving again, vanishing without a ripple. ✢

Looking at loons is like looking at a disaster movie from the 1970s, one of those summer shockers in which the sun goes wild and destroys the earth. The only people who survive are those who are underground at zero hour, or in elevator shafts—somewhere protected from radiation and light. One day, the loons are floating on some Cretaceous lake. The duckbill dinosaurs on the shore are trumpeting to their young. Sound is echoing everywhere in sonorous calls and hooting and whistling and piping. The loon dives after fish, and when it comes up again, the world is silent, empty. Only the loon is left to break the silence with its cry.

Whenever a loon watches me I feel—well, not judged, but measured. A perfect physical wisdom, the whole presence of life on the earth, is watching me. ✢

Loons easily make the journey from air to water and back again, as if there is no surface to the water and the worlds of trees and stars scarcely differ from their reflections. A loon swims in and out of its dreams, chasing silver fish. It goes deep into its body and finds its name. ✢

At mating time, an air drenched in the blossoms of wild roses blows over the lake. For kilometres along the shore the rich clouds and banks and solitary bright fires of wild roses bloom in shades of pink and red, some dark as a woman's lips, some bright as the wild geraniums in the grass, some as pale as evening snow. The lake is a pool made of condensed clouds that have fallen drop by drop. The whole cleft in which the lake sits has been dipped in a crystal decanter of perfume, then lifted out and set in the swooning yellow light. Drenched in that perfume, the loons mate in an elaborate dance. First, the male chases the female by calling excitedly and running across the bay. The two of them leave long, white trails like jet boats. The chase stills many times, then suddenly takes off again in another direction, often dipping underwater. After tumbling there under the sheets, so to speak, the birds erupt from the lake in a shower of spray, then chase off again.

A lot of birds are noisy out on the lake while they are mating. In the blue morning fogs of the spring, when every leaf and twig along the shore gleams dully with the pewter dew of the cold nights, the calls of grebes, ducks, and mergansers come from all points, swirling through the mist. The whole lake becomes a big speaker stack booming at an outdoor rock festival. None of the birds are as visible as the loons, though, and none of the others turn a serenade into a triathlon: running, swimming, *and* diving. It's not exactly Romeo below Juliet's window in the damask rose garden, but pretty much—you get the idea, I'm sure. ✦

*A*nassa paddled the canoe for the first time when she was seven. It took all her strength just to hold the paddle steady as she drew it back through the water. From the pollen muck at our shore, where frogs' eggs covered with algae bobbed among the reeds, we steered out over a long shallow pan of boulders and yellow clay. Halfway out in the lake, we went suddenly cold as the bottom fell out from under us. On that darkness, every fleck of willow cotton, and every mayfly, burned like a thread of tungsten. Slowly, as the trout leaped into the air and splashed down again, the ripples spread out in silver rings, each ring wider but dimmer than the last, until the black, smooth face of the lake returned to stillness, only to be broken somewhere else, then somewhere else again, slowly, measured. The clouds burned two feet under the surface, the only light in a dark world. The lake was black. On that darkness floated the seedheads of dandelions, and at times a bee, pointlessly lifting its water-sodden wings and dropping them again. The occasional mayfly had gotten itself trapped there as well, with its curled tail and its wings like the wings of a faery in Arthur Rackham, in a plate set into a book by hand. ✢

The lake is an eye, staring out of the earth, an eye without consciousness behind it. The canoe cuts across that eye. ✢

The year after I moved to the Plateau, I had the stirrup in my left ear replaced with a short length of titanium wire. Together with the hammer and the anvil, the stirrup is the smallest bone in the body. It's scarcely longer than a grain of rice. It looks much like a wishbone that you pluck from a chicken and wish upon, tugging at it with your daughter, or your father, as the case may be, but a whole lot smaller. I tugged and got lucky. The surgery was a success and I could hear again. Beethoven, who suffered from the same form of hearing loss, should have been so lucky. He should have eaten more chicken.

There's a downside, though: the surgery destroyed my sense of balance for a month. Two weeks after surgery, with only the rudiments of vertical hold, I walked down through the afternoon wildflowers to listen to the terns with my new ears.

As I shuffled down, I cut the perfect figure of a thirty-five-year-old Canadian man in worse shape than a seventy-year-old Swede on skate skis. Above me the siskins moved soundlessly through the branches of the pines, small, grey-brown birds scarcely bigger than the cones among which they moved. They were about the size of a small child's fist plunged first into a tub of honey and then into a tub of feathers. They hung upside down, immune to gravity, shifting from cone to cone like crabs. As I tottered up to the trees they seemed so still, but when I got close and stood for a moment to catch my balance and slowly looked upward to watch them, the whole tree was suddenly full of this movement, for its entire twenty metres of height.

Actually, the whole world was full of movement—and it wasn't the world; it was me. After a few minutes, I got my bearings. Sick to my stomach, with Leandra skittering away in front of me, I slowly, unsteadily, walked down to the lake through the flowers and the moving trees, walking as I had watched Anassa and Leandra walk when they were eleven months old—like a pile of bones stacked on top of each other, the movement of each bone deliberate, overcompensated, corrected and balanced. I stepped down to the lake and sat on a rock at the edge of the water, as ants crawled over my feet and Leandra splashed, and I listened to the terns, using their calls to measure the return of hearing I had not known since I was fifteen-years-old.

And I heard them. I really heard them. The terns made high gurgling rills, as if they were blowing through tin kazoos trilled with their tongues. I went back the next day, and on the days after that. Each day my hearing improved—and my balance with it—and the whole time the terns never stopped. This life in the air is their life, regulated only by the rising and setting of the sun and the turning and tilting of the earth away from and towards it. Out of the endless movement of those algorithms and mazurkas, screeching through tubes of horsetails crushed flat and blown through shrilly, with Beethoven's curse behind me, I heard the terns with my new ears and stood up in the yellow sun and walked slowly, matching Leandra's tiny footsteps. ⁂

$\mathcal{D}$eep in the summer, the terns rebel against the loons. It's a full-scale revolution, but without machine guns and rifles and the Czar and his kids murdered in a basement. The terns aren't Russians. The terns pull their revolution off without a sound, and nobody gets hurt.

Suddenly a loon will rise in the middle of the bay under an arching blue sky that looks like a blue bubble of breath, held and trembling. Before the loon is properly out of the water, with periscope down and flotation tanks trimmed, a cloud of terns is there, riding over it, close, like torpedo bombers coming off a carrier deck. They swoop at the loon again and again, forcing it to dive. It does, slipping into water that closes over its head like silk. In this attack, the loon is like a gopher in one of those arcade games where a child pays a dollar to strike again and again at plastic gophers that pop out of holes in a table painted like a green field. The loon comes up again, and again and again, and again and again, for a half hour, until the show stops as mysteriously as it began. The terns flash off among the mosquitoes to their young—hanging in their nests like astronauts in their sleeping bags, strapped to a wall in the shuttle as the earth spins around and around below, like a ball in a game of roulette in Las Vegas. ⟶

$\mathcal{A}$long the shore in September, the bull thistles open in vast white clouds on spiny stalks almost three metres tall. Sparrows and chickadees feed on the black seeds, while the fluff drifts across the entire north shore, catching in white masses on the water, where the waves drive it against the willows. It catches in my parsley, too, sticks to my green beans, and blankets every patch of bare soil in my garden and in all the other gardens in back yards along the lake. The days are hot and yellow, and the nights are chill, as the first stars of winter precipitate out of the flower carpets of summer nights.

The heaviest concentration of thistles is at the Watson barn, a giant barn with a glimmering, blue-grey zinc roof, sitting as big as Noah's ark along the highway on the big northern bay of the lake. Before the Great War, Colonel Watson built it in the wilds of Western Canada to house a team of twenty-four Clydesdales, giant horses with moon discs for eyes and ocean waves tossing in their hair, and feet like the great, iron pistons of steam engines. To do the same feat today would mean moving to the wildest reach of the Mongolian or Russian Steppes and setting up a ranch there.

Eight kilometres away, the colonel built a spreading mansion for his true love from Scotland. She refused to come; the colonel shipped off bravely for war at the railway in Kamloops and was killed shortly thereafter. The barn, too huge to be truly useful for any other purpose, stood empty from his death, home only to swallows. The mansion had a brief revival as a communal house in the 1960s, with mattresses on the floors and endless parties and free love amidst the mosquitoes. Thirty years ago it burned to the ground. All that is left of the Colonel's dreams is his barn. In the 1980s, the tin roof was torn out of the grass, hammered straight, and re-laid, the beams were reset in the walls—or replaced if they were rotten—and the stalls were all rebuilt with new timbers. The barn serves now as a piece of history for tourists and the site of barn dances, medieval fairs, and picnics. The swallows are still there, though, streaming out of the open gables of the old haylofts, winging out in shimmering swarms over the turquoise water of the July lake, when the thistles and the algae are in bloom and the wild lilies, yellow with orange throats, are cool honey along the shore and in the blue shade under the trees.

The light from the barn's weathered doors carries only a dozen feet into the interior passage, dimming suddenly in an upright line. When I first stepped into that wall of brown darkness, the dim outlines of the barn leapt up before me and the big stalls opened up on either side. Swallow nests hung from the rafter above me, and swallows swooped in and out, fast, close to the heavy, two-inch-thick boards of the ceiling, dipping into and shooting out of their nests as their young chirred and skittered. At the back of the barn was a pair of Belgian workhorses, tan, with white manes like cherry blossoms blooming among dark trees on a long ridgeline in fog. They were stamping down straw and sawdust and manure, and turned their heads to watch me from the beginning of time, with the eyes of the sea.

Who would have thought that this giant barn, two hundred and fifty feet long, made of twenty-four-inch logs a hundred feet long, would have been built for this, for the swallows, who weave the summer light—a monument to Captain Watson and his innocent world, stronger and more poignant than the military cemeteries of France and Belgium and the butchery that placed them there.

When my daughter's school was raising money to buy computers— before we all realized that computers were no guarantee of cultural literacy—we held a family fun day in the barn, with balloons and cotton candy, a clown, carnival games in each stall, a barn dance upstairs, and goodies everywhere. BC Tel offered lifts in their cherry picker truck. The Great Root Bear came from A&W in 100 Mile House. For one windy June Sunday that opened in sun and closed in snow, the barn was a riot of happy children and shrieks of laughter and the stomp of dancers and wail of fiddlers, and swallows flying in right through the strains of the dance, among the dancers, among the children and the balloons. Then the barn went back to its silence, and an eagle swimming through a clear blue sky. ✦

On a dead aspen above the bulrushes below Captain Watson's barn, an eagle sits in the storms of fall, waiting for fish, all the grey of the sky buffeting against him, hardly ruffling his feathers, so that when he turns his head he turns it against the full face of the wind, effortlessly, turning the whole wind. ✦

In August, the sharp sulphurous scent of blooming algae floods through the barn. Those are the days when the lake fills a volume of air much larger than the volume of its bed. It is a breath, exhaled, hanging weightlessly among the pines, filling the old smithy and ice house, the livery stable, and the tin-roofed parlour of the 108 Ranch Historical Site. The girls home from university for the summer, who dress in period costumes and lounge on the front porch, are sitting in the lake. When they stroll across the lawns with their parasols, they are walking through its waves. The lake fills the air right up to the Sucker Lake ridge. Traffic hurtling down the highway splashes through it, throwing it up in swirls of spray. It fills the tour buses that stop in a hiss of air brakes on the long haul between the Rockies at Jasper, and Tokyo via Vancouver. When they ease off again, a little of the lake goes off with them, hanging in the dim, blue air among the seats right to the edge of the Plateau, an hour to the south.

The lake itself is warm and marshy and covered in sulphur-yellow pollen. The spring carnival of the birds is over. The midway has folded itself back onto its trucks. Except for the loons, the birds have pretty well all raised their young. The few who still have any left after the predations of the muskrats, the eagles and hawks, and the cats and dogs, herd them among the reeds, rarely venturing into open water. They are terrorized. The rest pretty well go their own way.

One of the carefree birds still wandering around in memories of the hall of mirrors and the big Ferris wheel is the grebe. I saw him one summer day, a comical-looking fellow with a bright red, chisel-shaped head, a beak too long for his body, and curiosity like a cat's. The sun lay in a yellow film over the water and he was swimming through it. The clouds and trees, even the houses, blue and brown, high on the steep slope above the shore, were reflected around him, skewed through the spectrum into shades of dandelion and lemon, balsam root and calendula. It was like watching yellow-and-green TV. There was only one channel. The grebe followed his neck through the sun, like the exact opposite of an anchor following a rope as you throw it overboard, a comical film played backwards while the audience roars—and then he disappeared.

He had swam right through the sun and had vanished from this world. Grebe, my shaman. ⇥

The next day was Sunday. We all spent the afternoon out in the yard, moving through the sharp breath of the lake. Diane was trying to catch some sun, lying on a blanket on the cut grass of the lawn. The cat was twining around her head, trying to wake her up. The children were playing house—making cakes out of sand and mud—over against the shed. I was pulling weeds from the zinnias when I heard a chirping, singing noise from the tall, seed-heavy grass past the flowers. When we had moved there five years before, it had been just more closely trimmed 2-4-D–treated lawn. I let it go, watching the clover, aspens, and paintbrush move across it year by year.

The grass beside my elbow parted to reveal the cat, stepping out in his seven-league boots, with a 4-inch-long bright green grasshopper in his jaws. The cat didn't know what to make of this insect—and, frankly, neither did I. I had never seen one before that day, and I have not seen one since. The cat dropped it on the grass. It immediately began to trill, a noise that sounded as if in the body of this insect the grass had gone to emerald, sparkling like newly pressed sap. Translated through that insect intelligence, it had become music. If I had been asked to make music out of grass, I would have transcribed the movement of grass stalks, the way they sweep and weave in shadow and light over distance. I would have talked about mathematics, not about colour and sap. But then, I'm not an insect.

I stepped out into the knee-high clover and laughed and called Diane over, for the grass all around me was covered with those insects. There were hundreds of them chirping their bird-like bell tones in that small field I had let grow wild, and nowhere else.

After a couple minutes, both of the cats were prowling through the music like bad liner notes. Diane and I quickly trudged back to the lawn, each with a cat in hand. We put them inside. By this time, the cats were frantic, and clawed at the window to get back out. We left them there to get over it and went out and lay back together on the edge of the lawn, listening to the soft music of the insects, as the sun hung in the air like a breath of vaporized wood.

The wonders were not over. As I lay back on the blanket, breathing the lake, I saw a white ribbon, like a long narrow battle flag at Acre, swirl and flap at the tip of the pine tree twenty metres above me. This narrow, wind-tattered flag was made up of tiny motes of light, like no-see-um flies or drops of water shining with brilliant silver in the direct sun. The pine tree was pouring its life force into the air, like a radio beacon, or a red aircraft marking beacon on the night hills—a spume of light so bright and thin it almost was not there, its light tossed and shifted by the wind, except there was no wind.

As Diane slept and turned red against my shoulder, I watched the essence streaming from the tree for half an hour. When my shoulder got sore, I eased out from under Diane's sleeping head and walked out into the tall grass among the giant insects and the flowers, and watched the tree from there. Once I had learned to see it—just as the heron is only visible in the spring once you have seen him move—the stream of light was always visible. All the time, the little brass songs of the insects rose out of the grass like Adam's name for the grass itself. The sun continued to soak into the earth, becoming more and more solid with every moment. There seemed no limit to the amount of sun the earth could absorb. ⤳

The sun comes in many different forms on the Plateau. In April, it comes as a big furry bumblebee as long as my thumb, burrowing into a small pile of sand beside the driveway to build its nest. In May, it comes as a cloud of yellow and black hornets, exploring every crack of the outside of the house, looking for a way in, butting up gently against the walls, again and again and again, then flying backwards, moving over two inches, and trying there. It makes a sound like a slow, hard rain. It goes on for weeks. The tulips open in the garden, spread their petals wide, then fall away in a flash of pollen and withered black petals, and the wasps are still trying to get in, testing the house like technicians crawling over the space shuttle in its hangar, hooking up hoses, inspecting insulating tiles, polishing up the paint, tiny against the vast flanks of the machine. During that whole time, the sky has grown a deeper, more resonant blue. Whenever I've left the door to the house open for a moment, one of the wasps has flown in. It's dangerous. It's like having small, remote-controlled cruise missiles in the house. They fly high against the ceiling, or flash and whiz at head level through the length of the house, before they settle in the screaming, molten heat that lies against the windows, and fly up and down against the glass, wailing, light trying to return to light. ⤳

When the pine trees bloom, the tip of every branch, from the largest limb to the tiniest twig, ends in a thick, yellow candle of pollen. Winds of pollen stream off the trees like yellow rivers flowing out of a wall of perception to suddenly materialize on the shore. Big rivers of pollen flaring along the lakeshore fill the air from the ground up as far as I can see, moving past steadily—an Amazon River of pollen.

Out there, watering the violets and flax in the pollen one March morning, as the cats slipped through the bushes after birds, I caught a flash of movement in the biggest of the pines above me—a wasp, hovering over the tree, shifting from candle to candle. Once I had focused on it, I saw another, and another, and another—then the whole tree swam into focus, like one of those Magic Eye books you buy for your kids. The kids bring the pages up to their noses then slowly pull them away until the random squiggles come into view as dogs and houses and leaping porpoises and fast cars. The tree was like that. Suddenly I saw wasps on every branch. From the ground to the high, stubby crown, the entire tree was alive with wasps, gold and flickering. ❖

The previous time I experienced a tree in this way was in 1977, on an orchard above Okanagan Lake. I was working in the glowing heat, thinning apricots on a point of land that fell away through the sharp scents of sage and clay to the lake sixty metres below. As I perched on the tip of the ladder, flicking small green apricots into the grass, they thunked against the steps of the ladder then fell into the sky. With the sky above me and below me, I often lost my sense of balance—it was impossible to tell what direction was up and what was down. There was no gravity other than the feeling of taking flight, of moving horizontally out into that air like a swimmer pushing off into a warm, blue sea.

Every morning and evening that summer, I changed the orchard sprinkler lines by carrying twenty- and thirty-foot-long two-inch aluminum pipes forty feet through the tall grass and the trees, then hooking them back together again. Line by line I made my way through the orchard in the soft *click click* of the sprinklers. After reassembling the final line, I dipped over the side of the cliff, on a steep and dusty tractor road leading down to a pear block in a hollow by the lake. I had driven the tractor over it so many times that the clay had been ground down into fine, white flour ankle deep. It was like walking on the moon.

The first part of the walk led down through a two-acre field of sweet peas gone wild, a carpet of bright colour spilling down around a giant ponderosa pine, its long needle-brushes sprouting in delicate tufts from its scaled limbs. The first of the path's series of switchbacks, zigzagging across the face of the cliff, turned just before the pine tree. The evening air was heady with scent as I came down around that bend. Golden, pink, and orange clouds streaked across the sky. Every evening, my mind was on the clouds, and every evening a male hummingbird, buzzing and screeching and hammering loudly like a Stuka bomber, dived on me at incredible speed, then pulled out of the dive an inch above my head and flashed up again, green and red and gold, before diving again. Each time it took me by surprise, and each time it was terrifying. Half-covering my head, half-looking-up to see the hummingbird—guarding his nest in the lower branches of the pine—I hurried down the path into the blue shadows of the pear trees to chamge my sprinklers, and then to stand in the shallows by the willows that rimmed the bay. For a few minutes, the soft waves washed against my skin, then, overcome by restlessness, I climbed the trail back to the orchard. The whole valley was in shadow by this point—only the sunset was burning with light, soaking the dark world. The pine tree had become a dark column rising out of the ground, and all intention—indeed the focus of the entire world—was directed upwards to the shining sky. In the poor light, the hummingbird did not fly anymore, and the sweet peas had lost their colours, but I walked up through their scent, completely alone, and at eighteen years old I knew who I was upon this earth.

Later, I sat on the grass under a pear tree outside my cabin, and as the sunset faded through lilac to violet to just a rim of deepest purple along the outlines of the clouds, I read Virgil under the pear tree. As the world quieted from the day and I quieted with it, I heard the bullsnake— a giant, four-foot snake with which I shared the orchard—slip in a soft, prolonged rustling through the grass. A light evening wind rustled in an ancient, inflected grammar among the black leaves of the pear tree, and when the stars rose out of the air and a sliver of moon crested the Gold Hills, it was Virgil's stars and Virgil's moon, and I was lost deep in time, drunk on space. ⁂

The next spring, I was living in an old chicken coop on the shores of Cawston Creek, a blind creek that runs down in the shade of Cawston Creek Canyon, but quickly dribbles out among the prickly pear cactuses of the benchland. For two months that spring it flowed in excess, rushing past my chicken shed, sounding like a Tibetan temple bell on the shale.

I spent my first six weeks on that farm using a hydraulic post pounder mounted on the side of an International diesel tractor with no power steering. My employer had just bought the old André's vineyard above Similkameen Station; it was my job to pound each one of the ten thousand cedar posts of the vineyard down an additional six inches, so they could last for another year or two. It was brutal work. I had to wrestle the tractor in close to the posts—on a sidehill, jammed between two narrow grape rows, without power steering. Then I had to smash the posts down by raising and lowering a small hydraulic lever mounted under the tractor seat, and it took up to twenty-five blows per post. Twisted and bent and wrenched out of shape, I did the work, my head cranked over my shoulder, as the hard metallic clang and deep wooden thud of the pounder rang out over the roar of the diesel. Out of my blue cloud of pounding and dust, my curses flooded down over the vineyard, where a young woman, Diane, who would in two years be my wife, first caught sight of me—or, rather, caught air of me, and thought I was a total ass.

It was mind-destroying work, but at the end of it, after six weeks, it was May, blossom time. With my body aching and my mind bruised, I went out to graft apple trees. The trees had been unpruned and were a snow of white blossoms. In that cloud, with a sea of dandelions slapping at my legs, I worked, and the stillness, in contrast to the brutality of the job on the tractor, enraptured me. I found myself going quiet there, more quiet than I had ever been before. After two days, I had reached a depth of stillness from where the world passed me in slow motion. As I sawed through the limbs with my pruning saw, the sawdust drifted down into the grass, as if time had frozen into the solidity of space—and space was sliding past, like a glacier. I cut the scionwood, slipped it under the bark, nailed it with tiny cigar box nails, and painted it with tar, and every motion was completely still. All around me there was the hum of bees and the scent of apple petals in the air. Petals and sawdust filled my hair. My hands were black with tar. When I took a drink of water to ease the heat, the stream spouting out of my wineskin into my mouth was silver. The sunlight was woven of strands of music among those trees. In all the branches that lay around my grafted, many-armed stumps, bees worked over the blossoms, as if the branches still reached up into the air, and throughout the rows of the orchard, robins called, like bells of juniper wood, and pecked at the rotten apples on their carpets of old leaves.

I had finished Virgil the summer before and had moved on to Pound's *Cantos*. I pulled that big, orange book out of my pack at coffee time, and there, under the trees not yet grafted over, I lay an old apple out beside me, starchy and wrinkled and sweet, a cup of liquorice tea, and Pound, and brought that whole valley into the moment of reading that book. After the pure transparency of the grafting, among new green leaves dappled with light and shade, the sun soaking the pages was almost blinding. In the scent of the sun on the hot, dry soil under those trees, I knew immediately what it was like to no longer be fighting a war. ✈

Six years ago, I dug up a pussy willow from the 110 Mile swamp. I parked my truck on the side of the road, slid down off the soft shoulder, through big boulders and the last salty old snow pushed off by the snow ploughs, and stomped through the muck, water, moose droppings, and still-frozen ground to a pussy willow sprouting with tungsten light among the bulrushes and the gnawed-off dogwoods. The pattern of frozen and melted ground was completely intermingled in that swamp. It was hard going. By the time I was finished with my shovel, I was smeared with deep, black marsh from head to toe. Slightly less enamoured with the job than when I had first slithered down the bank, I dragged my bush back up the hill and planted it in my own garden.

After six years, it is now two metres high. It started to bloom early this year, opening its glistening silver catkins in half a metre of snow. By late March, the catkins were five centimetres long and bright with yellow pollen. I went out one afternoon to prune the bush back so that it will bear an equally lush crop of catkins next year, and to keep the pollen down for the sake of Diane and her allergies, but when I got up close, I saw that the bush was alive. Tiny bees, a centimetre long, were working over the flowers. One solitary mourning cloak butterfly was opening and closing its wings in the warmth of mid-afternoon. The cloud of bees was the model of a giant atom in front of me, the synapses of a thinking mind, clicking and singing. I had seen into the creation of the world. I took my clippers back in. They could wait. ⟶

I learned waiting from the bohemian waxwings. They come in the first hush of snow, a swirl of flakes like the edge of a vast presence past the rim of our world. Their feathers puffed out like little down jackets, the waxwings shift quietly through the white soapberries under the aspens, clearing them off in two hours. Waxwings are social birds—the whole flock feeds together, but only a quarter of the flock feeds at any one time. The others wait in the bare tops of aspens. Every five minutes there is an exchange—the birds that are feeding fly up into the branchtops and the same number fly down to take their turn.

Of the hundred species of birds that call the 108 home, waxwings are one of the handful that stays for the entire year, foraging widely to get enough calories to keep warm under the green, winter skies. They know their territory well, and move from feeding site to feeding site. And so they come, not for the saskatoons in July, but for the dried saskatoons in September, and again for the soapberries in November, and the apples from my crabapple trees when they are frozen and soft in December. In May, the waxwings are out in the saskatoon field, eating the blossoms off the bushes. I bring them close with the binoculars, and there they are, huge, within my eye, on a spray of white petals, as the skirr of the yellow-headed blackbirds comes in from the swamp, like a violin made from a split old board that had lain out in the mud for twenty years. In January, they come for the rosehips, small red balls of fire in a streaming white world. In all that time there are whole months when the sky closes in and the earth is no more than the earth—all connection with the larger universe is cut off. During those months it is impossible to even imagine stars at all.

The stars again appear one night as a high wind shreds the clouds. To stand out there on a night like that is to feel that the world is at the bottom of a river in which float specks of silt and grit washed down out of a mountain by a fall rain. The water is so cold it takes the breath away and squeezes in on the temples like a C-clamp you use to repair a chair in the workshop after it started to give out at Christmas, but the eyes are clear, and you inhabit your body again, your entire body, and reach out with it.

Out on the water, the first snow falls through the still, black face of the lake, as if it is a black hole leading straight through the earth, with the big flakes drifting down, clear, for a few feet before dissolving. A week later, the flakes lie on the new ice. A month after that they have piled up high, while the bohemian waxwings are still slowly and gently making their way across the land. Creatures of trees and air, they never touch the soil, preferring even a foot-tall rosebush to the ground itself, bending it over with their weight, the red bark of the stalk glowing in the snow like molten iron. ✢

Early in my second Cariboo winter, I stood among the scattered willows as the stars dipped and swam through rags of cloud. The first new ice was breaking up among the reeds like a thousand little bells of cut crystal, making a paper-thin music that passed through the forest with the sounds of a party heard through a window in the night. Thin shards and flakes of ice caught the starlight out of the air. Driven by the wind, it built up into a white foam around the edge of the lake. The baby lay in my arms, wrapped in an old sleeping bag with ring-necked pheasants in the red lining. There, in the cold air, under the moon, she drifted into sleep on the small clouds of her breath. The houses on the far side of the lake were dark.

As I walked her past the point of the lake, under aspens chopped down and scarred by beavers, an owl fell out of the tip of a half-dead tree above us, catching herself on her wings and floating without a sound. We walked into the owl's silence. Suddenly she was there, in a tall, dead aspen above the bulrushes. The moon floated behind her shoulder, huge and cold, rimmed by tiny prisms of broken light. The owl watched me without blinking and all time vanished. She stared at me for a million years. When I finally turned to go back in, the baby's long, black lashes lay on her cheeks like combs made out of owl feathers, hushed, breathing the moon. ⤳

*A*s the big flatbed trucks roll south in the rutted asphalt of the highway with eight-inch square beams to be sawn into lumber in Washington, I think of my cat Nickel, who left us one early December night by vanishing without leaving even one track in the new snow. I walked through the aspen forests the next day calling, but there was no answering cry. In the afternoon, I stood on the edge of the saskatoons and said, "Good-bye, Nick," speaking to the air, knowing there would be no answer, speaking only to send my words out.

It was Palm Sunday. The Plateau was covered with blue smoke, pungent and marshy. I walked along the lake through that smoke, where the dead, high grass and the sharp thistles that were higher than my shoulders in October lay crumpled, their stalks broken at awkward angles only a foot above the ground.

It was an owl that got Nick, I'm sure of that, probably the one I saw silhouetted against the moon out on the dead tree on the point, staring at me out of a stillness I could scarcely imagine. When she stared at me

I was being watched by the entire night. Then she glided away on silent wings. It made her seem like a ghost, as if she existed in two worlds at the same time, as if through her I saw out of my world and into a world of spirits.

She showed up for nights in the pine above our house, calling. On her second-to-last visit, Nick disappeared in the first snow. That night, I had put the cats out at midnight into a sea of stars. In the morning, Nick was not there, and only one set of footprints led through the new snow out to the shed where the cats slept, and back again. Those were obviously Mac's, Nick's brother's, because Mac was there crying to come in. Nick's footprints led down the stairs from the deck, then disappeared. Either he had been beamed up into a UFO, his mission as an anthropologist here on earth completed (and knowing Nick, this could be a possibility), or an owl had got him in the night. I say an owl, because no coyote footprints led through the snow of the yard. There was nothing. It was an immaculate ascension.

The next night, the owl woke us, hooting in the pine at two in the morning. Diane and I lay awake together listening to her call, the tubular, rounded sound floating through the house, in every room at once.

In the morning, Mac came in with two round, half-inch deep puncture holes, one on each side of his chest. The owl never returned. Mac might have been the runt, but all those years of being pounced on by Nick had taught him how to squirm, all right. ✣

I met owls again at Mahood Lake. Mahood Lake lies at the eastern edge of the Plateau, fed by the Canim and Mahood Rivers, which tumble down deep horseshoe falls in basalt cliffs and wind through forests of white birch and salmonberries into the chill water. Rimmed by cedars and back-faulted mountains, framed by thirty-metre-tall cottonwoods and stalked by bears, Mahood Lake takes the full force of an east wind blowing interminably down its length. Its water is always dark. Waves crash incessantly at the shore. The first two yards of the lake are a scum of cottonwood seeds, seed casings, and scraps of sticks picked up by storms. Just past the far end of Mahood Lake the Plateau falls off to the Thompson and the rush to the sea.

The girls—four and nine—and I had gone out camping on Labour Day weekend, our last weekend together before Anassa went back to school for the fall. Diane was already back at her school, polishing her timetable, filling out budget and staffing forms, preparing for the first day of classes. The weather was hot. The girls and I had talked a lot about this trip and had agreed to spend our time on the lake and hiking up the Canim River. It was a good plan, with a little something for everyone.

The only thing that got in our way was the bear. Driven down out of the high country as the berries shrivelled up in the hot weather, he was roaming through the campground like Mel Gibson in a car chase, disappearing into the shadows only to reappear on the other side of the campground, agitated. He was a very grumpy bear who found the presence of people a great irritant and the presence of food a sorry temptation. All day the camp warden whirled around in his pickup, trying to head the bear off towards a bear trap baited with a well-rotted salmon, which stood off on an access road leading into the cedar bush. The bear was not going to have anything to do with that, however; come on.

As that fish-hating bear prowled angrily down the length of the river and along the lake, a merganser and her brood breasted the waves. With their brilliant white feathers and flaming red beaks the colour of chokecherries, they looked like a flotilla in the 1910 Kelowna Regatta. I counted seven young birds and two adults—it had been a good summer. As the big brood surfed up to the dappled water close to the shore, they began to feed, jabbing their bills rapidly. In a flash of light before them, I saw hundreds of tiny fish, scattering in all directions, leaves of light skittering over the wave-washed gravel of the bottom. The mergansers quickly spread out in a line and pushed closer to shore, feeding more and more quickly the whole time, as the cornered fish bunched up more and more densely upon each other. After ten minutes the birds had had their feed and my legs were numb from standing still in the icy water. The cold didn't seem to bother the girls. As the mergansers swept around the boat launch, crows stood on a lump of bark and wood, about six metres from shore, rising and falling with the waves, watching, too, taking note, filing it God knows where. ✣

I first met the bear at the outhouse. I was coming out. He was rooting around in the garbage cans outside, and demonstrated to me his method of opening what were supposedly bear-proof containers. I quickly slipped back into the outhouse before I realized that that was silly—the door opened inward and was held shut by a simple hook and eye. So I stepped out again. The bear looked up at me, and we came to an agreement. He let me walk off to the left. I let him eat his garbage in peace. He was a big bear. He was like a tightly coiled spring.

It was with unease that I sat beside the campfire that night, sipping peppermint tea. The darkness was intense. There was no moon, and the stars spread across the sky like a meadow of spring flowers. The sky was so clear, I felt as if I could count every star in the Milky Way, arching blue and white, yellow and red above the tall, black towers of the trees. The light from the fire only penetrated about three metres into the darkness, and much of that, at the edges, was very dim, before the night swallowed it. The dark had real shape, mass, and presence that night. What's more, it was full of a bear, which might come crashing out, huffing, at any moment, to put me in my place.

Then the owls came. The first one sent my heart racing. It was perched in the crown of a tree no more than a dozen metres from where I sat in my pool of light, with a few sparks from the fire drifting up beside me. I felt like I was sitting on an opera stage in Milan. The spotlight was trained on me and I soon would have to sing. I didn't see the owl, but that didn't matter. He was damned easy to track just by the sound of his cry—a loud, piercing bugle-cry, half howl, half ghost on the clarinet. After five minutes, when my heart had stopped racing and the opera patrons had settled down in their seats, he repeated it. This time an answering call came from farther out in the bush, perhaps three hundred metres away, and again my owl answered. It was a conversation I had no part in. I walked to the dusk at the edge of the firelight and, as its shadows flickered gently on the grey bushes beside me, tried to locate the owl against the backdrop of a million million stars. The trees were only dark gaps in the starlight.

The darkness was too intense to see a thing. For hours that night, I lay in my sleeping bag, the girls asleep beside me, listening to the owls talk across the crowns of the forest.

In the morning, I saw the bear again. This time he was loping rapidly through camp. When he saw me, he barked, like a warning shot fired across a ship's bow, and took off up the road. That afternoon, the conservation officer moved the trap and caught the bear at last. We could hear him for half an hour, banging against the walls of the cage, metal clanging against metal, rocking the cage on its wheels, before he was towed away. ✦

Ten years ago I sat at this window and wrote down the colours of the lake to form a palette out of which I could forget this late language and

learn the secret names of water and wind. Now I am a stranger. I have
come to listen as only one grown strange to his own home can listen for
the sounds a trout makes when sleeping, a star sings when swimming
down through the green of a leaf into the blackness of the night, a lake
breathes when the sun strikes it and does not find it there, but finds
instead only one large, silver fish drinking the sky out of the cupped
mouth of the land. Deep within my breath I hear the sound of geese
lifting off in a long trail across the face of the water and then the swell
of the ripples behind them for hours, stilling. After hours of darkness
without breath, I hear the low touch of Diane's skin as she sleeps, her
breath slipping in and out like a bird carrying stalks of grass out of a
meadow of clover and paintbrush in which it sings its children its songs
of travel and return. In the most beautiful love poem in the world, we
have the voices of a man and a woman on this cold earth, the sun is a
scent of trembling wind, and low fog curls over the spring gravel like
rain in a day of white blossoms hanging heavy to the black ground. This
is not the most beautiful love poem in the world, yet the birds cluster in
the pines outside and the whole house is filled with their jubilant return
after the months of owls, when the trees cowered in their roots and the
black hounds of the moon had free rein over the aching land. What we
have shaped is the simple touch of her lips to mine, the brush of her
hair across my face in the dark when we stay awake for an hour together
with all the lights off, and our hungry petal-soft breath. I love this house,
where her hair smells of the oil that gloves every inch of her—breasts,
arms, ankles, and the back of her neck—and with which she anoints me
and brings my mind to flowers which I would not otherwise see. This
bright house of children, birds, and flowers: we knew we would come
here from the first moment we met, and hid it from each other as hard
as we could for many years so it would be almost a surprise to be here

tonight, singing together like trees holding on to our roots, tight, in a strong wind. She is called black tern now. I am called night loon crying over yellow water.

March 29, 2001 ➜➜➜

Woody and Winston

a postscript

You cannot prevent the birds of sorrow from flying over your head,
but you can prevent them from building nests in your hair.
   ⁂Chinese Proverb

Ten years after we moved to the lake, we left and moved into the trees an hour north at 150 Mile House. Diane had taken a job with the School District Office in Williams Lake, and we had to weigh the pros and cons between living at the lake and the girls actually seeing their mother for more than a half hour a day. It was no contest, but it was the hardest thing we'd ever done.

I thought I had lost the birds, and in truth, during our first year up at the 50, I didn't have much to do with birds. I spent nearly all of my time in the basement, turning a concrete hole in the ground into liveable space. After a year of sitting on my step ladder at one and two in the morning, staring at problems of carpentry, sketching angles on scraps of Gyproc, thinking things through, trying to figure out how the whole jigsaw puzzle went together, I had learned five construction trades, and was done. I was proud, but exhausted. Then I got outside again. ⁂

It was a forced exodus; a woodpecker had been eating my house. She started by clutching the side of my study window and peeking in sideways like a cosmonaut peering upside down out of Mir on its last mission before it was sent down out of orbit to burn up like a big Hallowe'en sparkler over Australia. The woodpecker was eighteen inches tall, with a red cap and a big three-inch beak. She looked like she had just materialized out of a cartoon, circa 1967. My friends and I used to watch those old Woody Woodpecker flicks a lot, on our black-and-white RCA that beamed out from its big, maplewood chest while we lay on the linoleum floor and munched popcorn and the wind picked the house up and shook it to see if we were still inside. We were, shaking with laughter. Woody made us howl, with his ability to send up authority in any guise. In our houses of authority, he was our own personal shrink.

Woody also made me nauseous. I was a farm kid. Watching TV for a half hour made me feel as if I had spent the afternoon riding up and down in a green elevator between the observation deck and the turbine room of the Grand Coulee Dam, over and over again. After the show was over, I'd get up and go out and play with the dog. He smelled of stars. That was a lot better.

Well, Woody came back. This time she was female. This time she was not funny. She wasn't ha-ha funny, and wasn't, well, funny. You know. She was just nuts. She was hungry and she wanted to nest. Well, sure, I could see the humour in the situation, because it was too ridiculous for words, but it didn't make me shake with laughter, either. In fact, it brought out the worst in me. This time I had to be the authority figure. This time I had to lay down the law. This time I had to be the wicked witch out in the forest making my house out of gingerbread, then locking up the woodcutter's lost children for eating it. I mean, really. It's too much. I felt like Elmer Fudd.

So, I took to pounding on the wall and yelling, and scaring Woody off that way, and it worked: she leaped away from the house with a big swoop of her white-and-black fringed leather Harley biking-jacket wings, and snapped her claws into the fir tree outside the study window and laughed at me from there, "Ha-ha-ha-Ha-ha, ha-ha-ha-ha-ha-ha-ha!" Well, back in the cartoon it was laughter. Out here, outside of that maple box, it sounded like she was as frustrated with the way things were going as I was. She had a nasty glint in her eye. ✦

I started out thinking how blessed I was to have been visited by such a beautiful bird. Forget all that. I have been watching too many loons.

After three days of fluttering, interspersed with sharp pecks at the glass of the window like the bangs of a carefully aimed brad hammer, which always made me jump, I tell you, Woody threw the gloves off. When I drove home from town that day, she swooped in front of me from tree to tree in her characteristic wave-like motion. "Great," I thought. "Just great. Hitchcock."

It was prophetic. As I came around the front of the house with the mail and a bag of groceries, I found a pile of wood splinters along the walk. I looked up, waaaaay up. I started to yell. Woody had eaten the lower frame of my window, right down to the weather-stripping set into a groove in the centre of the wood, and had taken the upper corners off the window frame as well. By the time I put the groceries away and came back out, Woody was back at the window. Each time she smashed down with her beak, and then pried sideways like a carpenter with a crowbar working over a couple of 2 x 4s, a splinter of wood two inches long and a quarter inch thick went fluttering to the ground, where it landed with a small click.

By the end of the afternoon, I had stapled plastic dropsheets over the window, white and yellow and maroon from my monkish months in the basement. To get them in place, I balanced on the top step of the neighbour's eighteen-foot extension ladder and reached up to my fingertips. I made sure Diane wasn't home, so she didn't have to watch.

Woody landed on the plastic as soon as I stepped down off the ladder, but leapt off again in a hurry and yelled at me again from the fir tree. "Fine," I thought. "Yell."

People had lots of advice. "Hot sauce," one friend said. "They hate hot sauce. Paint that on and she'll stay away."

Hey, I was game. I had hot sauce. I didn't have the world's hottest hot sauce, but I sure as heck had the world's second hottest hot sauce. A friend had sent it up from the Midwest as a joke. When he had visited the summer before, Leandra had stared him down and told him that the spoonful of Louisiana hot sauce that he fed to her was not hot at all. The girl's got spunk. This new hot sauce had her in pain for a half hour: *Insanity Sauce.* Good thing she only had a couple drops. It was perfect for the woodpecker.

Over the next few days, I carefully reconstructed the window. I cut out lengths of wood, squared up the holes, shaved new wood to fit, glued it in, filled the cracks, sanded it, repeated as necessary, stained the whole works, and then, as a finishing touch, painted it all with a nice thick coat of take-you-to-hell-and-back hot sauce. "Try that!" I said to the air.

Woody did. I believe Woody is a Mexican woodpecker. She looooves hot sauce. The next morning, she smashed out all my spliced wood, all my crack filler, and had made inroads on the window halfway up the frame—all within an hour. The concrete down below was covered with three-inch splinters of wood. I picked one up: the first half inch was bright red from the hot sauce/salsa dip; the rest was the white of new, knotless wood. It looked like a match. Give Woody a pipe and she could be Popeye's gal, Olive Oyl. Oh, this was really getting out of hand. ⇥

$\mathcal{W}$ithin four days, I had plastic on seven windows of the house. Study, garage, bathroom, bedroom, it didn't matter: Woody went for them all, only moving on to a new one after I had stapled plastic to her current project. With the house wrapped in plastic, like an old onion twisted into a sheet of Saran Wrap in the fridge, it was time to get serious.

That afternoon, I went on the Internet. I found out a lot about pileated woodpeckers, real quick. The most important thing I found out was that many people give up. The birds are endangered, so you can't shoot them, and the birds are persistent—more persistent than humans. "Well, it's no wonder they're endangered," I thought. Duh.

"Cover the hole with wire netting," was one suggestion. Over a window? Not.

Another article suggested hot sauce. Right. Well, at least the guy had the decency to suggest painting it on again daily. Give him that.

"Build her a house," said another article. "She's looking for a home, so give her one. Perhaps she'll leave yours alone."

It was worth a try. ✢

I now have the most beautiful woodpecker/kestrel/barn owl nest in town, made according to the rigid specifications of the US Forest Service. I borrowed a twenty-eight-foot extension ladder from Jerome, who lives down the road, so I could nail this little avian villa twenty-four feet up on the southwest side of a tree. Pileated woodpeckers love the southwest sides of trees (and houses), and really like things about twenty-four feet off the ground, like my study window. That's another thing I found out that afternoon in nowhere land. They also like a particular shade of brown that you used to be able to buy out of the Sears Catalogue and which they called "Peanut Butter." When you bought it, you earned Airmiles. Buy enough and you'd be on your way to San Francisco, to buy fish down on the docks, and maybe a tour of Alcatraz to see where the bird man hung out, why not. My windows are painted that colour. It really does look like peanut butter.

My woodpecker house is painted that colour. Woody found it all right. She pecked all around that house, flipping off chips of bark from the fir tree and sucking up the bugs scurrying underneath. She refused to go inside. ⇥

*W*hen Woody smashed the backup mirror on my camper, I just had to laugh. She must have seen her reflection in there, gotten territorial (Internet again), and given it one clear, clean, well-aimed punch with her beak, like a cold chisel and a ball peen hammer. Pieces of mirror lay all over the ground.

By this time, people were giving me a different kind of advice: creosote, sling shot, shotgun ("Harold. If you can arrange to be away for an hour, you might find that the woodpecker won't be bothering you at all when you get back. I don't know how. I just feel that might be the case."), leg-hold trap. They were beginning to look on me as a disgrace.

I was determined to live and let live. It was becoming a battle of wits. Poison seemed too simple, and, besides, it would kill the beauty that still lurked somewhere inside that demented bird.

I was also discovering friends I never had. This was definitely not the first woodpecker to have terrorized a house on the Plateau. When I talked about it, people's blood pressure rose. They got awfully passionate. They told me about siding and netting and 5:00 AM and tin sheets and that damned hot sauce that didn't work for them, and they told it to me twice if I didn't stop them. I could relate to that. I'm sure they could have told it to me three times, easy. Interestingly, all of the areas of attack were painted brown. A word of advice: skip the brown next time, folks. If it looks like aged wood, it, well, it looks like aged wood, and you don't want that.

In the end, I fell back on a couple of old farmer's tricks. I drove into town, bought a tube of tanglefoot paste and all of the shiny Christmas ribbon I could find down at the dollar store in Williams Lake: eight rolls.

"Is this all you have?" I asked.

"Hmmmm," said the manager, pulling out a box from a bottom shelf. I peered in with him. "There's this nice ribbon here." He held some up: satin, bright colours.

"Very pretty," I said.

He shrugged. ⇗

*T*anglefoot is a sticky substance you can apply around the trunk of a tree to trap climbing insects. You touch that stuff and you're either stuck (if you're an insect), or are trailing long spaghetti-strands of sticky goo wherever you go (if you're not an insect). The more you try to get it off, the more it spreads. I didn't think Woody would like that. She struck me as being very particular. I nailed strips of wood to the bottoms of all the window sashes, and painted them with the tanglefoot. Step one.

The Christmas ribbons had worked to keep deer out of my father's young cherry trees below the Indian Reserve in Oliver. Deer are skittish of sharply flashing slivers of light. Woodpeckers are skittish. You see the connection. Step two.

Right. Well, I cut the Christmas ribbons into metre-long lengths, climbed up Jerome's twenty-eight-foot extension ladder, and stapled the strips to the tops and sides of all of my windows. Even the slightest touch of a breeze caused them to snap and flutter and cascade with light. By the time I was finished two hours later, the whole house was rustling, as if rain was pattering on the roof and flowing down the gutters. Flashes of light were spilling through the rooms. Over and over I was tricked into thinking that someone had just opened a car door in the driveway and had sent a windowful of sun splashing through the house in a big nuclear flash. I would run to the window. No one. I was alone with a bird. ✦

The ribbons were murder on Diane. She'd lie in bed for hours at night, unable to sleep because of the incessant rain. All through the hot weeks of July she woke at dawn, thinking the heat had finally broken and some rain was falling on the parched, dusty soil. Half asleep, she'd lie there dreaming of cool water, moss, and robins hopping across the grass. When she got up two hours later, she'd open the windows to tinseltown. Big letdown. As for me, I'm half deaf. No problem.

I left the strips on for three months. All that time, Woody yelled at me from the forest every time she saw me in the yard. Anyone else could walk out into the yard, could walk down among the trees, could do pretty well whatever they felt like, but if I so much as showed my face around the corner of the house, where Woody could see me from her nest in the poplars out back, she told me off right away.

She kept it up right to the end. When I brought the ladder back from Jerome's to repair her damage in the fall, long after I thought she had gone south for the winter, she snapped at me from the trees out back as soon as the rungs of the ladder met the wall. She's been watching me pretty close, I'd say.

Next time, I'll be ready. I have an extra-large roll of ribbon put aside for the spring. As soon as the snow melts I'm going out there. It's a pretty nice looking house, all-in-all, and if it has to look like Christmas for the whole spring and half the summer, what's it to me, eh? I like Christmas well enough.

Woody doesn't. Grinch. ✦

Never ones to leave well enough alone, we bought a dog. Well, we didn't exactly buy him. The SPCA pretty much paid us to take him away. He started off as a ten-week-old puppy of eighteen pounds with silky black hair, one crooked ear, and snowshoes instead of feet. By sixteen weeks, he still didn't come anywhere near to fitting his feet, but he did weigh sixty-five pounds, with no end in sight. It had become obvious that he had eaten the SPCA out of house and home. I took him to the vet.

"What are we looking at here for finishing weight?" I asked. You have to know how to talk about an animal like this. Simple human/pet terminology won't do. A pet like this is livestock. As I tell everyone who sees him for the first time, never underestimate a dog that leans against the fence and looks you in the eye.

"A hundred and thirty pounds," said the vet, "give-or-take."

What do you call a dog like that? He looks like he was put together by committee. His tail is too fluffy, his ears too small, his nose too long. His father was Akita. His mother was Newfie and Shepherd. Sometimes he looks like a stretched Newfie, like one of those limos hanging around the airport like sharks around a beach of margaritas and neon-coloured sunblock. Sometimes he gets a glint in his eye and looks like the Big Bad Wolf out of *Little Red Riding Hood*. At times like that it's best simply to leave him alone. Other times he just looks like a bear. *Bear* seemed too obvious. He has a big heart. *Shakespeare* seemed too presumptuous. We finally settled on *Winston*, after his jowls came in and he took to hanging his pink tongue out of the side of his face like a cigar. ⯈

When Winston was a year old, he started to have a thing about the ravens. Whiskey jacks he just gave up on. They swooped down out of the trees and stole his food one piece at a time. It didn't take Winston long to realize he would never catch them and would never be able to do a thing about them. When they come now, he just lies on the dust/snow/ice/mud/needles in front of his pen (there must be a word for that stuff), and watches them out of big, sad eyes. The eyes might be big, but they're set very close together in his face. He really does look like a bear. At first I thought I was going to have to spray paint *DOG* on him during hunting season, to keep him safe. I keep him in his run instead. Any dog with a long-distance gait like Winston's is just not a candidate for the open range. What with all the cattle, deer, and moose around, he wouldn't last a week. ⟡

One November day I went up to Latremouille Lake, on the edge of the Plateau above Little Fort, to see the wild rowan trees one last time before winter. They are no taller than a ten-year-old girl, and small and thin, but they are sacred trees. The place is sacred.

I was too late. Up there, winter had already begun. In the six inches of snow, the red berries of the rowans gleamed and burned with colour and fruitfulness. Being there was like being in the orchards again, in that old sense of sacred land brought to fruit, but with one important difference: this fruit was wild. This land did not bring fruit because of human intervention. I wanted to bury myself in the snow and become a bird and live there. I wanted to be those trees rising into that light and the gleam of the fruit. All I could do with that tension was to laugh out loud.

The whiskey jacks laughed, too. They swooped out of the trees when I cut open an apple, a Belle de Boskoop with its mouth-puckering skin and honey-sweet juice, one of the precious few I save each fall for moments like this when each bite becomes the air in my mouth. The whiskey jacks hopped across rocks and fallen logs. They swayed on the ends of the rowan twigs. They got most of my apple.

Whiskey jacks get most of Winston's food, too. Sometimes he looks at me so sadly when they come that I know he considers them like mosquitoes, very large mosquitoes: unbearable, but unavoidable. Sigh. ⇢

The ravens are another matter altogether. With the ravens, it's personal. The ravens, you see, go after Winston's bone. We're not talking about just any bone here, either, but about the two-foot-long cow thighbone Diane brought home for Winston at Christmas. We got goose with all the trimmings. He got a slaughterhouse. Seems fair enough. He was happy with it, anyway, although I'm pretty sure he would have liked both the goose with all the trimmings and the slaughterhouse.

I took Winston for a lot of walks during the two weeks past Christmas that year, trying to shake the goose fat out of my system. On those walks, I began to notice that when the ravens croaked in greeting as they flew overhead above the trees, Winston grew agitated. He got more than normally agitated. When he caught sight of a raven out of the corner of his eye, his head jerked sideways towards it, and he gave it a hard glare, and hurried up his walking pace. I had to scurry to keep up, before I could haul back on his chain and check his gait.

One day a raven flew overhead just as we were entering our yard. Just like us, it was heading straight for Winston's pen. Winston was beside himself, so I unhooked his leash and let him go. He took off like a British football fan after a referee. I was right behind him when he rounded the corner into his pen, and there I saw the ravens, standing around Winston's bone like Indiana Jones and a bunch of his archaeologist buddies around the Ark of the Covenant, discussing how to take off the lid without scratching the gold. Winston exploded into the middle of them and they hopped up lightly into the trees, then flew away laughing into the bush. They would be back.

When Winston started climbing over the fence around his pen, I electrified it. As I said: livestock. I need a saddle. ✣

$\mathcal{S}$till, Winston gets out sometimes, and when he does he runs madly off into the bush to terrorize whatever wildlife he can find. I take it seriously, because it's against the law to terrorize wildlife. And for good reason. I don't want animals to drop dead from exhaustion while goofy old Winston, pumped up on Natural Source Large Breed Adult Dog Food, runs them down, hardly working up a sweat. I don't want the conservation officer, or a rancher, plugging him between the eyes. There are moose and deer out there, ravens, rabbits, squirrels, foxes, coyotes, crows, grouse, and geese. Of all of those, geese are the most fun. Geese make noise.

When Winston got out one evening last spring, Diane found him by following the noise. He was in the middle of a goose swamp surrounded by sedges and bulrushes and one muskrat house like a geodesic dome on Saturna Island, chasing a pair of geese from one end of the pond to the other. The pond was about a hundred yards long, and Winston was right out in the middle of it, churning away, head and shoulders out of the water, bearing down on the geese. By the time Diane got there, the adult geese had herded their goslings together, putting up a defensive screen around them while they made for the reeds. Things looked grim.

They weren't. When the geese got near the end of the pond, the goose slipped off to the side with the goslings, while the gander flapped his wings dramatically and made even more noise than before, honking and hollering and hooting and hissing. He was tremendous. Winston suckered right for it and increased his pace. While the goose and the goslings slipped off through the reeds to the side and away from the pond, the gander led Winston up onto the muddy shore away from her. Just as Winston crawled, exhausted, out of the water, the goose slipped back in and paddled for the other end of the pond. And away they went!

Winston followed that goose through ten circuits of the pond like that. He was sinking lower and lower in the water, and his pace was dropping off. Things really did look bad.

"If I hadn't grabbed him when he got to the end of his run, I think he would have drowned," said Diane. Later, she also told me about the mosquitoes that really liked living down around that pond, and how they had really appreciated her showing up at the end of an otherwise pretty uneventful day. She could still laugh, though. That was a good sign. Malaria was not setting in just yet. "After he shook all his slime and water off on me, I told him that it was really, really, really sad when a goose is smarter than you are."

"What did he say back?" I asked.

"He stuck his tongue out at me and said, 'Let me at them again. I'm sure I can catch them.'" ◆

$\mathcal{W}$rong. So, it's the inaugural match of the Canine–Avian Chess Championships, and Winston the Attention Deficit Hyperactivity Disorder Contender is competing against Squawk and Klook, the raven pair from the trees back of the Harley hangout three streets along (they do *so* like it there). First move: Squawk plays a feint (she dodges behind the doghouse, where she can't be seen). This is a secret protocol to the main match, and Winston misses it, because he's been sticking his long, pink tongue down through a little hole he's drilled in the ice on his water bucket, stretching it out thinner and thinner until it makes a little pink ladle with a handle fifteen centimetres long, drawing it back up with water, extending it, drawing it, extending it, like Jean and Chere Lisa in

Trois Rivières, fixing a hole in a bucket with satire and straw: it all takes time. Lots of time—not an endless length of time, but lots. Winston *does* see the second move, though, bless him, the one in which Klook stands in the middle of the pen, waves his wings over his head, and calls out, "Hey, Dog, here! Hey! Dog! Whoooooooo!" Oh, man. Winston is off! Chess has never been played like this. And Winston and Klook are racing to the bottom of the pen thirty yards away, Winston doing the greyhound, and Klook swooping in a broad arc that carries him past the back fence into the neighbour's trees and around in a big circle. While they're down there and Winston is imprinted again with the concept of chain links, Squawk makes her move, sidling out and happily downing those doggie bites like a robin slurping down popcorn worms one after the other. And it's now Winston's second move, and the big guy doesn't hesitate! He barrels back all black and pink with white teeth like ivory-handled fish knives and white eyes ablazing like the cover of an old copy of Jack London's *The Call of the Wild.* Squawk's move. She flaps up in a big arc, down around the bottom of the pen and into the neighbour's trees, while Winston slathers on the chain link, prances around like Northern Dancer warming up for a big race, and Klook starts chawing down on those good little nuggets in Winston's dish. And, I know! Let's do it all over again! This goes on for ten minutes, until Winston stops in the middle of his pen as if he has just struck a radio-controlled dog containment fence, drops his tail down, lowers his head, and looks like he's going to cry himself away until there's nothing left of him but a gumboot, because Winston has just figured out that the ravens are smarter than he is, and that hurts. That really hurts. ✦

Round Two. This time Winston has two full food dishes, as it has just been feeding time, and, well, they don't make dog dishes big enough for a guy like Winston. You know those dog toys they sell by the aisle down at Pets R Us? Those balls on ropes and those tennis balls with neon-coloured bones stuck through them like some hand-drawn, hand-coloured cartoon of cannibals and missionaries? Five minutes from introduction to digestion. No lie. You know those nylon leashes, bright purple, turquoise, blue, or pink, for taking your best friend out for a tour of the local hydrant scene? One week. He even ate the seatbelts out of the back of my Honda. All three.

"We'll replace them for you three times," the insurance adjuster said. "After that, you're on your own." He's been around. You gotta like that in a man. Even so, that does mean I pay the deductible: $300.

Gee, thanks, Winst.

That's what the boy's used to, though. What he's not used to is this: Squawk is standing expectantly a foot away from Winston's food dish; Klook is standing two yards away from Winston; Winston is standing in the middle of his pen. His head and ears are down, his tail is sagging, and he's not moving. He looks a mess.

I yell at the ravens through the bathroom window, "Look what you've done to my dog! You've broken him!" I really think so, too. I really think I'm going to be living for the next decade with a broken dog, like a garage-sale-special Game Boy missing its joysticks.

Then I notice that Winston is moving. Winston has obviously kept his big brown eyes on the hunting cats these last few months. He knows the moves. With his head looking *away* from Klook (clever!), because, as everyone knows, if you don't look at them they won't think you have any interest in them, no way, he makes little cat-like movements, ever so slowly, towards the raven. I say cat-*like*, because Winston doesn't have such great fine motor control. When he was a puppy, it was like watching a boy in front of a glass case full of stuffed bears, popping in a loony and trying to catch a bear with a crane, jerking around on a joystick that really had little to do with what happened to the crane at all. With the cat thing it is worse, but in an endearing way. All Puss in Boots, over a span of five minutes, Winston edges up to within a metre of Klook. All the time, of course, Klook just stands there, staring up at the sky, sometimes whistling, sometimes whispering under his breath, "Come on, Dog. Make my day!"

And the dog does, and they are off, Winston doing the barrel roll and Klook doing the curl around the back of the fence through the neighbour's trees, and Squawk chawing down. After ten minutes of this merry-go-round in a tea pot, Winston stops like he has just hit a brick wall, droops his tail, sags his head, I turn away, and the ravens put that food away like there's no tomorra. ➷

$\mathcal{R}$ound Three. Tomorra. Winston is eating out of one dish in front of his doghouse. A yard away, the ravens are eating out of the other dish. ➷

$\mathcal{R}$ound Four. Diane calls me to the bathroom window, where she's been folding towels. "You have to see this!" I put down the onion I'm slicing for dinner and hurry back to have a look. Sure enough, I *do* have to see this. Exhibit A: right hand dog dish; full. Exhibit B: left hand dog dish; empty. Winston is eating out of Exhibit A. Squawk and Klook are lined up behind him in single file, waiting their turn. ➷

$\mathcal{R}$ound Five. It's 11:00 in the morning and I'm shovelling snow— twenty-five centimetres of deep wet snow that, unfortunately, turned to rain at 1:00 AM and kept up like that all night. It might only be a dozen centimetres thick now, but each shovelful is like lifting a Christmas duck's weight of water at the end of a metre-long pole. This is not the way a simple machine was meant to be used. Winston's tied up by the porch, so he can bite the snow whenever I pass by. It's pretty fun, all right.

I've been at it for about an hour and a half, which makes me a bit more than halfways done, when one of the ravens lands in the fir above me, and calls out in greeting, *Kalook!* I shovel away and call back up, without looking, "Hello, friend!" The raven, however, is not in a social mood, and keeps calling, more loudly, and more insistently, "Hey! You! Human! Food! Now!" I lean on my shovel, my breath rising and falling heavily, and glance his way. Klook's staring down at me from ten feet up. This is definitely *not* textbook behaviour for a raven.

But with a look like that, I get it right away, I tell you. I nod my head lightly, and trudge off to the pen. Klook follows me from tree to tree, scalloping lightly between them like a man stringing out an extension cord for Christmas lights.

In the pen, I fill up the dog dishes, and call out, "Dinner time!"

Klook says, "Thank yooo," respectfully. Winston doesn't even work himself up into a flap. He's made his peace. ✦

*M*e too. Well, sure, when I was a kid, my mother once cooked us up a dinner of starlings that my father had shot down off of the power wires by our apricot orchard. I remember picking them up for him out of the dust. I was the bird dog of the family that afternoon, and at dinnertime our mother served us tiny birds in gravy. At least we didn't sing a song of sixpence.

After that, I thought it was a great idea to go out and catch birds. My father probably thought it had been a good solution to the bird problems he was having in his apricot and cherry trees. He was eager. It must have been my mother who put an end to it. After all, she is the one who had to pluck all those birds: all those feathers for, what, a mouthful of meat? Knowing my mother, she wouldn't have stood for that for very long. ⇒

ℱorty years later I was picking cherries in Oliver with my father and his friend Marco, an Italian builder from Vancouver. As I was perched on the top of one of my father's aluminum orchard ladders, with my head sticking up through the top of the tree, among branches and leaves spattered with juice like a crime scene, Marco told me about his childhood in Italy.

"I used to build little wicker cages," he said. "Inside the cages I would put a few poppy seeds and a sparrow. We used to have poppies all over in our wheatfields there. It was in the Dolomites, in the mountains. There were poppies everywhere, growing wild. The poppy seeds have opium in them. When the birds eat them, they begin to sing. They don't stop, either." Marco started laughing in the tree below me. I descended down through the chainsaw massacre, back to the world of green leaves and thin shadow and the glint of sun filtering through onto ripe fruit. "When the birds came over the hills from Russia, on their way south to Africa for the winter, we were waiting for them with big nets. The whole village turned up. The birds came in big clouds right over the crest of a hill, following the sound of that singing bird. Just as soon as they came over the top of the hill, we threw the nets up in the air and caught them. We caught a lot of birds that way. It was one of the main things that we had to eat there." Marco was leaning against his ladder by this point, popping cherries off their stems with his teeth and chewing on them while he talked. His smile was red and bright. His eyes sparkled with melancholy.

My father's bird scare started up. Normal bird scares are pistol-launched bangers or natural gas cannons that go off at set intervals—at a hundred or even a hundred and thirty decibels. Dogs hide. No kidding: when farmers first started using the prototypes of those things back in the 1960s, they used to scare the daylights out of me. The birds' nerves were frayed by them as well. Every time a banger went off, they jumped up out of the trees like kids bouncing on a trampoline, flashed over to a different part of the orchard, and settled down again. Each time they got more jittery, but they never really left. Once they got used to it, they didn't even jump anymore. In fact, they didn't even raise their heads. Farmers really got into it after that. In the 1970s, Similkameen Vineyard used to have a trapline, with bird traps set up on top of posts among the vines. You had to watch where you put your hand. The farmer used to prowl up and down the rows with his shotgun. It was best just to try avoiding stealing grapes in that place.

Then came the Maseratti of bird scares. This sucker has a loudspeaker mounted on top of a seven-metre pole, and on five-minute intervals bellows out a terrible screaming cry over my father's orchard. It starts out with the high scream of a red-tailed hawk, then the distress calls of robins, blackbirds, starlings, blue jays, and woodpeckers. After a couple hours out in that, the orchard feels like a scene from *The Killing Fields*. It does keep the birds out of my father's cherries—except for that last row of Bings by the pine trees. That appears to be fair game.

"They still go hunting for birds there like that," said Marco, shaking his fist at the bird scare. "But they don't catch very many any more. The birds just aren't there anymore the way they used to be." He said it sadly, wistfully. He brightened up. "Your dad should try that here," he said. "Instead of that machine!" Juice dribbled out of the corner of his lip. He laughed and wiped it off with the back of his hand. "These cherries are sure good! These are the best cherries I've had in my life. In Vancouver we can't get cherries like this. Why not?"

I laughed. "They're only good right off the tree."

Marco nodded, and reached for another clump. ✧

*W*hen I was helping Marco load his cherries later in the afternoon, I saw a robin hopping through the trees. I asked my father if there were any birds eating his cherries.

"Just in the Bings," he said. "The bird scare keeps the rest away. It cost me $280, but it was worth it."

"What about the robin?" I asked.

"What robin? There's no robin."

I laughed. "Yes there is. I saw him there ten minutes ago."

"Oh, he must have been in the Bings."

"He wasn't in the Bings, Dad. He was eating the Vans right by the bird scare!" Those young Van trees were my father's pride and joy. I figured I had him there.

"Oh, him."

Oh him. Right! Ha! "I thought you said there were no birds in the cherries?" I feigned innocence and surprise. God, it must be tough to have sons. They never give you a moment's peace.

"There aren't."

"Yes there are. There's that robin!"

"There aren't any except that robin, but he doesn't count."

"How can't he count? He eats cherries just like any other bird." Oh, this was fun.

"Yes, but he doesn't eat very many. He lives here. He's not a wild bird."

And so the story came out. Two years earlier, when my father had set up the bird scare, one mother robin had already laid her eggs in a crotch high up in one of the big, old cherry trees. When the bird scare started up with its dive-bombing attack on Rotterdam, she had nowhere to go, so she stayed through the whole invasion. There must have been three hundred birds torn apart piece by piece around her every day that summer as city by city fell in front of the Luftwaffe. Her nerves must have been shot.

Her kids, though, knew no other world. It's like a pregnant woman playing Mozart so her unborn child will grow up with an appreciation of music, and might calm down and stop kicking her in the ribs, too, thank you very much. Those robin chicks grew up all grey-skinned and prickly-feathered in that bombing attack, just like any other war kids. They weren't bothered by it at all.

"Now his grandkids are starting to come back," my father said. He shrugged.

We each come to our own wildness in our own way. Late that night my father admitted that in about five years that bird scare was not going to be any damn good at all anymore. ✦

Every spring the loons come to Kokanee Bay on Lac La Hache. The lake was once used as the annual gathering spot for the Secwepemc people. They gathered there for weeks in a party of food and athletics and Lahal, the stick gambling game of the Northwest. While gambling and telling stories, people would get together and settle the political affairs of the whole nation. After it was all over, they broke up and went their own ways back home, family by family, village by village. The lake wasn't named by the Secwepemc, though. It got its name from the early French-Canadian fur traders, who came up from the Fraser at Soda Creek, crossed the Plateau, and went down to the Thompson at Little Fort, before continuing south to the Similkameen and the Columbia River. One of them found a tomahawk in the water along the shore: tomahawk, hatchet, la hache. The name stuck.

The town also calls itself Lac La Hache, and announces itself to the world with a long narrow sign, "Welcome to Lac La Hache: the longest town in the Cariboo." The town stretches for twenty kilometres along the lake, sometimes spreading itself out thin into a ranch and a few houses among the trees, sometimes clumping up into subdivisions, even settling down at the south end of the lake into a tumble-down collection of houses around a collection of gas stations, a town hall, three motels, a Swiss restaurant, and a diner. Kokanee Bay lies about halfway along. At its south end is a tiny Indian Reserve. It can't be more than two acres of scrubby willows and billboards, one of the reserves set aside not to live on, but to fish from. The fishing was once good. There's a picture at the 108 Ranch Historical Site, right next to Colonel Watson's Barn, of a woman in the 1920s skating across the ice to scare big, twenty-pound trout into the shallows where her brothers were waiting to spear them. The fishing is now done south of Kokanee Bay, opposite the cafes and gas stations. At the beginning of the winter, men tow their ice-fishing shelters onto the ice with their pickups and leave them there a hundred yards offshore. They say you have to drive at just the right speed on that lake, so that the wave of ice pushing before you has time to move out of your way. They say if you drive too quickly, you ride up on top of it and break through.

All winter, the men and women of Lac La Hache jig for trout in those huts. The trout come in at about eight inches. By spring, everyone's freezers are full. The trout are packed in there like anchovies.

Most of Kokanee Bay is skirted by the Kokanee Beach Resort, a motel/trailerpark combination with a big asphalt parking lot out by the road. Across the road from the Kokanee Beach Resort is Clancy's Restaurant and Gas Station, decorated with a shamrock and offering down-home cooking. It's owned by Koreans. Next to it is a sprawling log house, with a sign out front in German: Cariboo Guest House, $49 single. A Swiss flag flies from the gate. Lac La Hache has seen a lot of changes over the years. ⇥

Some things never change, though. Every spring, the loons come back to Kokanee Bay. While the resort caretakers are raking the lawns by the water and setting sprinklers on them to green them up for tourists, even as the snow is still lying old and rotten under the trees, the ice leaves Kokanee Bay. It leaves from there before it leaves any other spot on the lake. In fact, the ice leaves Kokanee Bay before it leaves any other lake around. For a hundred yards out from shore, in a bay three hundred yards long, there is no ice. The water is cool and blue and catches the light, while all the rest of the lake is green with old, rotten ice. The lake glows. There is absolutely no question of going out on that ice. It would be suicide. Down at the south end of the lake there are usually one or two ice-fishing shelters that were not dragged back to shore in town, tipping crazily over in a slow, slow fall into the water.

Every spring, I go to Kokanee Bay to watch the loons. It is the grey time of the year, when I feel as if the whole world has gone to ash and I know in my bones there is no chance that life will return to a dead earth. I might know it, but I hope against hope that I am wrong, and that there will be a miracle. It is a nagging memory to me in the spring, that there will again be green trees and pink clouds of rose bushes and loons chasing eagles away from their chicks out on the open water with their voices alone.

And then I find the loons. They fill Kokanee Bay. I have counted a hundred and twenty loons there at one time. They swim in pairs. Some are a couple metres from shore, while others swim thirty metres out, at the very edge of the ice. There are big, curious pairs of loons, and small, skittish ones. There are loons that float in stillness, and loons that swim slowly past as if on parade, and loons that dive quickly, out under the green shelf of ice, deeper and deeper into the lake, and come back out again five minutes later, the water streaming off their heads like sound. There are loons that stand up on their tails and spray themselves with water and stretch out their necks and lift their heads into the light. The whole genetic range of what it is to be a loon is represented there, for five days every spring, in Kokanee Bay. Each year, I walk out past the sprinklers and the old man sweeping the parking lot with his broom, and stand on the grass to watch them. ⟶

One morning, the ice falls into the lake, and in a few minutes the whole winter is erased. It seems as if it had never been.

The loons disappear that morning. They swim off to all corners of the lake, and fly off into the smaller lakes up in the hills, gone to fight the geese off of their muskrat nests, to see themselves into another year, and through it. Their excitement is palpable. It hangs over the lake for days. It hangs over me for life.

November 30, 2003–August 11, 2005 ⟶⟶⟶

HAROLD RHENISCH lives in 150 Mile House, BC. He won the Confederation Poetry Prize, 1991, the *Arc* Poem of the Year Award, 2003, and *Arc* Critic's Desk Award for best long poetry review, 2003, and most recently the *Malahat Review* Long Poem Prize, 2005. He has been a seven-time runner-up in the CBC/Tilden/*Saturday Night* Literary Contest and won the BC & Yukon Community Newspapers Association Award for Best Arts and Culture Writing, 1996. His non-fiction book *Tom Thomson's Shack* was shortlisted for two BC Book Prizes in 2000, and its sequel, *The Wolves at Evelyn*, will be published by Brindle & Glass in September 2006. *Winging Home* is his nineteenth book.

⇨⇨⇨

TOM GODIN is a writer and illustrator whose weekly birding column can be found at www.100mile.com. One of his drawings was selected to grace the T-shirt of the 2005 Baillie Birdathon. Tom began drawing birds incessantly after being inspired at an early age by the bird art of Allan Brooks and J.F. Lansdowne. After many years of studying his subject Tom's bird drawings underwent a transformation from scientific renderings to what he calls bird extrusions. The ballpoint pen drawings in this book are the results of that process.